What people are saying about

Ideology and the Virtual City

Videogames are gradually re ...)rm which reaches far beyond me ... ew forms of subjectivity and temp ... on with the new form should not ... that, in their content, even at its mo ... ..gic, videogames are firmly rooted in our neoliberal capitalism and faithfully mirror its antinomies. This is where Bailes's book enters. Through a detailed analysis of selected games, from Grand Theft Auto to Persona, he demonstrates how they reproduce the key dimensions of a modern megalopolis: the City as Playground, as Battleground, as Wasteland, as Prison... *Ideology and the Virtual City* is not only insanely readable; in its combination of vivid descriptions with theoretical stringency, it provides an unsurpassable introduction into the deadlocks of our real life. In short, an instant classic for everyone who wants to understand not just games but our reality itself.
Slavoj Žižek

Videogames are the battle ground on which the culture wars are fought, and the space of gaming is shaping the political present and future, whether we like it or not. In this insighful and politically vital intervention, Jon Bailes reads the contemporary city through its representation in videogames and considers how city space itself is tranformed by games. Bailes shows how the city and the virtual world can hardly be separated, making a case for a critical-theoretical engagement with games which makes their politics, importance and limitations visible. A timely and important book on a topic so easily and so often misunderstood, setting the terms for future discussions of gaming.
Alfie Bown, author of *The Playstation Dreamworld*

Ideology and the Virtual City

Videogames, Power Fantasies
and Neoliberalism

Ideology and the Virtual City

Videogames, Power Fantasies
and Neoliberalism

Jon Bailes

Winchester, UK
Washington, USA

JOHN HUNT PUBLISHING

First published by Zero Books, 2019
Zero Books is an imprint of John Hunt Publishing Ltd., No. 3 East St., Alresford,
Hampshire SO24 9EE, UK
office@jhpbooks.com
www.johnhuntpublishing.com
www.zero-books.net

For distributor details and how to order please visit the 'Ordering' section on our website.

ISBN: 978 1 78904 164 4
978 1 78904 165 1 (ebook)
Library of Congress Control Number: 2018947800

A CIP catalogue record for this book is available from the British Library.

Design: Stuart Davies

UK: Printed and bound by CPI Group (UK) Ltd, Croydon, CR0 4YY
US: Printed and bound by Thomson-Shore, 7300 West Joy Road, Dexter, MI 48130

We operate a distinctive and ethical publishing philosophy in
all areas of our business, from our global network of authors to
production and worldwide distribution.

Contents

For Cihan

1

Introduction

In the final moments of the videogame *Persona 5*, one of its teenage characters, Ryuji Sakamoto, comes to the conclusion that, "If you want to change the world, all you have to do is just look at it differently." Indeed, by this point in the game the world has changed, primarily due to the efforts of the group of young rebels to which Ryuji belongs, with their ability to enter an alternate dimension formed from unconscious cognition to alter people's innermost desires. But even in more everyday circumstances, without such supernatural power, there is something relevant about Ryuji's sentiment, in that the first step to any social change is recognizing how certain assumptions underpinning our behavioural and ideological norms are contradictory or counterproductive. If we cannot shift our perspective towards an alternative view, we simply won't challenge these assumptions, and things stay as they are. If that seems obvious, what is less so is what it really means to "look at the world differently," because some ideas are so heavily entrenched in cultural processes and institutional structures it may never occur to us that they are matters of perspective at all. Even major disruptive events, such as economic crises, wars and natural disasters, may fail to shake the received wisdoms that connect much of society. In fact, despite Ryuji's observation, this problem of perspective also applies to him and his friends, who ultimately haven't changed the world as much as they think because they didn't consider the deeper causes behind the social issues they resolved.

This book is about some of the deeply entrenched ideas in modern societies, and how they may make it more difficult to properly confront widespread social problems such as poverty, oppression and environmental decline. It is also about videogames, and how they function as modern cultural expressions that represent different responses to and interpretations of those ideas. So what are these ideas? To begin with their form, or how they take shape and become part of our lives, I am in a sense talking about dominant ideology, yet not exactly a clear philosophy or set of political aims consciously propagated by an elite class (although that is one aspect), so much as a diffuse "atmosphere" that intertwines with everyday processes. In many ways it is the "common sense" that tells us what is expected of us and what should make us happy in modern societies, in areas such as work, leisure, health, property ownership and human relationships. It is not a command that we must obey directly or completely, but a set of unwritten guidelines in the "background" of social life, which we may internalize in different ways, depending on our particular personalities and circumstances.

As for content, it is difficult to give this background a definite name because it is often reproduced without ideological intent, by people simply following the routines of their daily practices. It also varies from one society to the next and within societies themselves, depending on the identities and cultural experiences of the groups that comprise them. Even so, to a great extent we can see this background as an effect of a particular economic reality that exists today with a level of consistency across the globe, in terms of the expectations it places on people in both the wealthier and poorer parts of the world. To this degree, the background which connects us all and which we all respond to psychologically, whether in support or criticism, is capitalism, and specifically the modern form of capitalism that can be loosely called "neoliberalism," whose notions of value have colonized our existence. Put another way, it is under the economic and political neoliberal orthodoxy of the 1980s onwards that a logic of competition, instrumentalism and unimpeachable market sovereignty has been gradually normalized throughout social life. This logic reinforces pre-existing notions about the necessity of wage labour and consumerist ideals of personal fulfilment. Yet it also tells us that, regardless of the social problems that remain, this is as fair as society will ever get, and it is up to us *as individuals* to realize the opportunities for success and satisfaction it provides.

Certainly, neoliberalism is not the only determinant of the "common sense" background ideology in modern societies, not least due to a continuing patriarchy that is also often deeply embedded in everyday assumptions and behavioural norms (and evident in the games examined in this book). But neoliberal conceptions are central to our daily decision processes, not to mention our understanding of what is politically and economically possible. Thus, even when people aren't happy, and want their lives or their societies to change, the neoliberal background still tends to frame the scope of their critical imagination. Seen through its lens of common sense, it is not neoliberal capitalism itself that is the problem, but the government for being too bureaucratic, or certain groups of people for demanding too much, or ourselves for not working hard enough to realize our potentials. And then, even where capitalism or neoliberalism clearly are the problem, the logic tells us that there is no better alternative anyway. But what if we reframe the way we view social problems by looking at the demands of neoliberalism themselves? What if the particular pressures we experience to advance our careers, enjoy ourselves with consumer entertainment, accumulate property and construct an idyllic family life are the *causes* of dissatisfaction? What if they don't match an economic reality that increasingly makes it harder for many people to manage such feats? What if the onus on our own individual responsibility for our circumstances starts to feel less of an opportunity than a burden? Can we ask these questions and bring the ideological "background" into view by "looking at

3

the world differently" and imagining an alternative, or must our criticisms and complaints merely fold back into the neoliberal logic?

The other important question, at least in the context of this book, is what do videogames have to do with any of this? After all, the act of playing such games seems a far cry from that of challenging our most deeply entrenched political and economic ideas. The simple answer to this question is that videogames are cultural objects, along with films, TV programmes, books, paintings and so on, that in some way reflect the culture in which they are produced. If we want to understand how people internalize, justify and struggle with the demands of neoliberalism, they are useful representations, and as good a place to start as any. However, I believe there is also something especially significant in the way that many videogames function as power fantasies, which grant their characters, and through them their players, a sense of agency and control that they generally cannot experience in everyday life, whether saving the world from aliens or taking control of their favourite football team. And in particular, when these games are set in stylized representations of modern reality, as opposed to either being direct simulations or taking place in pure fantasy worlds or abstract spaces, they often seem to embody a desire to confront certain boundaries or limitations in society.

On the surface, the power fantasies in these games may do little more than indulge immature cravings, by offering opportunities for unhindered hedonistic pleasure and/or the violent disruption of social norms. But each also frames this behaviour according to some sense of an antagonistic force that must be resisted. If these games are escapist fantasies, then, they do not simply block out the drudgery or aggravation of reality but make the escapee work through it, albeit in an unrealistic way. Perhaps more than other media, it is this "working through" or attempt to resolve an antagonism through the player's participation that makes some videogames especially intriguing when considered as manifestations of different worldviews. Most interesting of all, in my understanding, is how they then function as *ambiguous* responses to neoliberalism. That is, they simultaneously criticize existing social conditions and reaffirm certain common assumptions about how the world works. In this way, it is not the question of their potential ideological influence over players I am concerned with here, so much as how the objective-centred, interactive forms of the games portray and symbolize the varied and complex ways in which people reconcile their experiences and desires with neoliberal demands.

In this book I focus on four games set in and around representations of modern cities. These are *Saints Row IV* (2013), *Grand Theft Auto V* (2013), *No More Heroes* (2008) and *Persona 5* (2017).[1] The American and Japanese cities in which their action occurs vary widely in their depictions, from liberating playgrounds to hyper-competitive battlegrounds, desolate wastelands and regimented prisons. In each case, the specific form the city takes can be seen as an interpretation of modern social conditions, and the challenges the players must overcome as allegorical renderings of contradictions or antagonisms in those conditions. For the most part, the result is not explicitly political, and certainly not intended to outline a programme for dealing with actual social problems, or for imagining progressive social alternatives. In fact, following the trajectory of some Marxist and psychoanalytic theories of ideology (most notably Fredric Jameson and Slavoj Žižek), I see the power fantasies in these games as largely *unconscious* attempts to resolve social issues that they cannot *explicitly* recognize or formulate. This unconscious undercurrent is often particularly noticeable in what videogame theorists call "ludonarrative dissonance," or a disconnect (intentional or not) between the personalities and motivations of a character established by a game's narrative and the actual actions the player performs as that character.

5

As games provide more developed characters and storylines, alongside a wider choice of activities, this gap between what they "say" (through scripted scenes) and what they "do" (through the player's agency) can become more pronounced, and provides a great source for identifying repressed meaning and unrecognized conflict.

At a basic level, all four of the games I examine here centre on their characters' quests for happiness in worlds that initially rob them of meaning, power or enjoyment. Completing the game by beating its ultimate adversary provides the solution, because in doing so the characters effectively overcome the obstacle to happiness that was manifested in the city. Yet these solutions remain fantasies, in which social antagonism is given the shape of alien overlords, supernatural beings, professional assassins or shady politicians and businessmen, rather than institutional inefficiencies or internal systemic contradictions. Even in the more "real-world" cases, where the adversaries are corrupt elites, the games do not connect their characters' dissatisfactions to hierarchies of power constituted by neoliberal political and economic conditions. Of course, these games never claim to be solving the world's problems, and have no overt pretensions to spark alternative political ideals, but the issue is that, because the deeper social issues they hint at are allegorized rather than consciously formulated, when they reach their endings and the fantasy antagonism is vanquished, they are never quite satisfactory. The characters may be happier than when the antagonism arose, but the "background" remains largely untouched, so the improved situation appears doomed to expire.

Another way to look at this is to say that such examples of commodified popular culture are often critical up to a point, but the way they define their adversaries and antagonisms remains within a commonly acceptable range that stops us really getting to the meat of the issue. On one hand, they contain clear themes relating to actual social problems, interwoven with varying degrees of nuance into the fictional narratives and structures of play they provide. Perhaps the most common such theme is that of finding a clear sense of purpose in the modern world, presented through characters plagued by an absence of meaning in a society whose individualist consumerist aspirations feel insufficient. In such representations, conformism to regular expectations of work, leisure and property accumulation is in some way understood as inadequate, as it is evident that either the promises of fulfilment are false, or that the social game is rigged against the majority of people. Without naming neoliberalism or capitalism at all in most cases, these characters reject its instrumental values, its demands on their behaviour and its notions of a "normal" life. They are clearly disillusioned by common sense prescriptions and the opportunities defined by neoliberal ideals, and desire something more.

On the other hand, what they desire *instead* reveals a failure to escape some of the deeper assumptions in the neoliberal fantasy. And so, with each of the four games I analyse here, I identify how they embody a different kind of psychological response to the ideological background, and consider how these responses both criticize the social order and continue to internalize core neoliberal ideas. In other words, these psychological responses or interpretations effectively "rationalize" the existing order as somehow fundamentally acceptable, or at least inevitable or unchangeable, despite its flaws. I define these four responses or "ideological positions" as "hedonism," "cynical self-interest," "escapist defeatism" and "reformism," and in each case explore how they reaffirm the neoliberal background even as they point to major problems in individual and social life. For example, the hedonist has little time for the notion of fulfilment through work and career progression, but internalizes the promises of consumer pleasures and the need to oppose the overbearing authority of big government; the cynic recognizes the extent of social corruption, but absorbs the neoliberal pessimism about human nature and collective political organization, and perceives individualistic competition as an unavoidable reality; the defeatist (also a kind of cynic) understands the absurdity of modern day social pressures, but accepts that the economic system is too powerful to challenge and cannot envision a better alternative, so escapes into consumer entertainment; the reformist sees social change as necessary and possible, but works to unblock particular instances of corruption, rather than questioning in the systems of opportunity and enjoyment or the goals they inspire.

My aim is to show how the ambiguity of these positions, as psychological attempts to reconcile neoliberal demands that are ultimately neither fully critical nor conformist, shines through in the games' depictions of society. It may initially seem odd to look for such ambiguity in these sources, since the games themselves are clearly pieces of commodified entertainment first and foremost, if not big budget culture industry products with corporate backing aimed primarily at mass (male) market appeal. Indeed, as a form of media, games in particular have grown up within an orthodoxy of neoliberal ideas and economic systems, having only really become culturally significant since the 1980s. More fundamentally, perhaps, the ways most videogames form objectives and make demands on the player create clear parallels with key neoliberal concepts. As videogame theorists such as Andrew Baerg and Matt Garite have argued, game structures often force players to focus on advancing their individual interests to reach a goal, and only *appear* to provide freedom to achieve this goal in any desired way. So, even when game narratives frame player decisions in weighty moral terms, it remains tempting to act purely based on material gains and losses. If the quickest way for my character to get a better weapon is to kill the friendly computer-controlled character (or NPC: non-player character) currently holding it, whether or not the game penalizes such actions I am only really obliged to consider the negative consequences for myself. In the end, because the overriding objective is to win the game, I am implicitly encouraged to calculate risks and rewards around personal advancement, which naturalizes an extreme form of individualized instrumentalism. At the same time, while games effectively address players as autonomous individuals who make important decisions, their main narrative paths are generally predetermined. The result is a kind of illusion of choice in tune with our consumerist freedoms to make purchasing decisions from a predetermined range of choices. In "open-world" games, especially, where players are allowed to roam large, non-linear environments and encouraged to "do anything," the array of possibilities obscures the underlying rigidity in the system of rules itself, and that all the choices available fulfil individualistic (and violent) desires. In fact, it can be said that videogames structurally embody the neoliberal concept that "there is no alternative." In the game, the lack of alternative is literal; we cannot act in ways not coded into it, and must either accept its systems or stop playing completely.

Despite all of these valuable considerations, however, a distinct "utopian" element also resides in many games, including those I examine in this book. In some cases this is intentional, but my focus here is on how the utopian element is often revealed precisely by a game's "failure" to identify social antagonisms in terms of the background neoliberalism. In each case there is a kind of residual dissatisfaction that is not resolved by the different characters' journeys, even to the extent they realize their aims of consumer freedom, individualistic success, escapism or social reform, precisely *because* there is a bigger issue, and the task still remains to define what that is. It is useful here to consider what cultural theorist Fredric Jameson once referred to as "cognitive mapping," and in particular how difficult it has become in today's societies to grasp within consciousness the infinitely complex workings of society or our own positions within it. This inability to effectively "map" and understand the cause and effect relationships between different social, political and economic phenomena is then manifested in cultural objects, which also cannot possibly represent the social order as a totality. But at the same time, Jameson tells us, a cultural representation in some cases "unexpectedly suggests the possibility of cognitive mapping as a whole and stands as its substitute and yet its allegory all at once."[2] That is, even in falling short and "only" managing an allegorical representation, the concept of *attempting* to create a cognitive map or really grasp social antagonisms is kept alive, and with it a demand for greater effort to comprehend the current reality.

In examining the games in this way, I am also trying to show how ideology functions in modern societies, in terms of both the neoliberal "background" ideology and a range of psychological responses to it that are not explicit political ideologies, but still revolve around certain beliefs and justifications. In this way, the four positions I look at here all effectively support the existing social order, yet not in the sense of following a clear political philosophy or doctrine. Rather, they illustrate a kind of ideological process that goes beyond sincere obedience to a specific creed, towards more of an overall psychological investment in things as they are that nonetheless has particular expectations and limits. In truth, neoliberalism itself is difficult to pin down as an ideology, because it does not *explicitly* demand obedience, but asks people to work out, realize and take personal responsibility for their own desires (always implicitly within a "free-market" capitalist framework), in a way which engenders varied responses. Many people's conscious relationship to neoliberal ideals thus tends to be ambivalent, and their acceptance of the existing order then depends on the extent to which they can "rationalize" its contradictions in accordance with their lived experience. Put simply, people are often committed to the neoliberal capitalist order *indirectly*, for example, as long as the economy works to provide for their needs or any alternative systems seem weak and ineffectual. But even those ideas are contingent on how people conceive of their "needs" and the aspirations associated with them, as well as notions of what alternatives are possible and what they could provide. What is *not* commonly perceived is that, in these attitudes, more deeply ingrained neoliberal conceptions (about the good life, individual responsibility and the lack of political alternatives) often *are* absorbed without question, and make the attitudes ideological in their own way. But also, since they are merely ideas, they can be contested like any other ideological belief.

In the next chapter I consider the concept of a neoliberal background ideology in more detail. I define what kinds of expectations or pressures it produces and how these filter into everyday life, as well as the logics supporting them and the antagonisms they create. I also describe how people deal with these contradictions through fantasies and rationalizations that they use to justify acting in line with neoliberal expectations. Each of the four chapters that follow is then dedicated to a particular videogame, and considers that game in terms of the ideological position intertwined in both its narrative themes and interactive structures. Certain aspects of these analyses, such as audio-visual styles, plotlines and character motivations, will be familiar to critics of other media, and are often equally crucial, especially in defining a game's overt ideological messages. But it is also necessary to consider how players interact with games to understand how they produce meaning that either reinforces or contrasts the explicit themes. As digital cultural theorist Lev Manovich has noted, for example, the way we move and act in the 3D space of games can itself build characters and themes, and I too consider how traversing the city space in these games creates different impressions and experiences. More generally, I am concerned with what videogame theorist Ian Bogost calls the "procedural rhetoric" at work in these games, or how their interactive processes either reproduce or question common assumptions in line with various ideological motivations. The common thread between the games examined in these chapters is their modern urban setting and their ambiguous relationship to it that neither fully celebrates nor condemns it. I outline the "power fantasies" (predominantly aimed at young males) represented in these games through their characters and their objectives. I also point to the contradictions that each contains, when seen as an ideological response to neoliberal demands, particularly between its expressed narrative themes and the actions of its characters (via its players). In the final chapter, I conclude by summarizing the features of each ideological response, but also consider how they all still seem to demand something more than neoliberalism can offer, indicating points from which a critique of the social order itself could grow. Or ways in which we might really "look at the world differently."

2

Ideology and Neoliberalism

If we are to consider neoliberalism as an ideological background in modern society, and the various worldviews we encounter as responses to it, we need to define more clearly what neoliberal culture actually is.[3] In particular, what kind of "expectations" does the background place on individuals, and how do those individuals interpret and rationalize any contradictions that emerge? First, I should reiterate, I am using the term "neoliberalism" loosely here, not strictly as the economic school of thought associated with economists such as Friedrich Hayek and Milton Freidman, but as a kind of cultural paradigm that has emerged from the rise into orthodoxy of this doctrine, especially since the 1980s. Capitalism is still at the core of this paradigm, of course, and specifically a form which promotes economic growth through business investment and job creation in a heavily deregulated global market. As the theory goes, individuals pursue their economic self-interest in a competitive environment that raises the standards of living for everyone, or at least everyone who is willing to participate. The result in terms of ideology is that this focus on competition and individualism valorizes self-reliance and the notion that each of us is responsible for our own financial circumstances, which we should naturally aspire to improve. In what Ulrich Beck calls the "risk regime", "people are expected to make their own life-plans, to be mobile and to provide for themselves in various ways."[4] Capital moves to take advantage of lucrative opportunities, and we are supposed to be endlessly flexible and continually reinventing ourselves to keep up.

Seen this way, it may seem that there is actually an absence of a clear culture that could be associated with neoliberalism.

Rather, we are bombarded from all sides by countless demands from different sources, such as the state, the workplace, our social circles and the media, with no unifying ideals to harmonize them. If anything, perhaps the sheer bewildering weight and incompatibility of these simultaneous demands to work hard, be politically active, invest responsibly, socialize regularly, stay healthy and keep up with cultural trends *is* the quintessential modern cultural condition to which we respond. But there is also a certain logic that connects these disparate injunctions: a kind of instrumentalism that converts all aspects of life into calculable values, and speaks to the individual as a consumer who can define his/her own life through hundreds of micro choices. In a sense, everything from politics to personal relationships is subject to this logic, as each decision apparently counts towards an individualized and commodified ideal of success and satisfaction. As such, it is not that there is no systemic logic, but that the logic itself creates a sense of both freedom and chaos, with a singular demand for individual fulfilment that is full of contradiction in practice.

The contradiction occurs because the pressure of success is limitless and covers every area of life, so it seems that we can never do enough, or that some of our efforts actually counteract others. Crucially, in my view, it is a mistake to view these varied demands as a matter of achieving "work-life balance," because encoded into the neoliberal ideal of success is a hidden clause that nothing is ever enough; we can always earn more, have more fun, own a bigger house, be more attractive and so on. Through the very attempt to keep up with the expectations of this logic, the goalposts continually move and fulfilment is permanently delayed. The question then is how people react to the contradictory pressures, and how they reconcile the gap between ideal and reality by prioritizing some demands over others or imagining ways that the ideal may become possible, given the right social changes. In most cases, such "rationalizations" still function within the confines of the background ideology, rather than considering the system itself as flawed. But that does not mean these responses are not critical of neoliberalized culture, or that they are without contradictions of their own.

With these concepts in mind, we can begin to understand the neoliberal "background ideology" more clearly and ask further questions. First, how are the expectations of modern societies presented to us as neoliberal ideals? As mentioned above, the logic of neoliberalism effectively reframes all aspects of life in economic terms of success and failure, or whether or not we are maximizing our range of personal resources for individual gain. Yet, as Jodi Dean points out in her analysis of neoliberalism as ideology, this logic is in turn framed as "freedom," specifically through a notion of "free trade" that constitutes the predominant neoliberal "fantasy."[5] In effect, the concept of "free trade" signifies the possibility that everyone in society can "win," as long as the market is freed from constraints and state interference. With that potential unleashed, it is up to each person to make informed, rational choices to take advantage of the opportunities available, so the deregulated market economy is associated with the formal possibility for *every* individual to create their desired lifestyle. Again, what is noticeable here is that this core idea pertains to an *individualized* concept of fulfilment, which disconnects the purpose of our actions from religious principles, national interest or collective social improvement. Instead, we are called upon to fulfil our personal potentials and invent our own sense of identity, or marketable brand.

In these circumstances, failure to reach fulfilment reflects back on the individual: freedom has been granted, so it is our own responsibility to realize our ideal selves (with self-help guides and life coaches available for those who can afford it). In effect, then, the universal aspirational idea of "freedom" is redirected towards a specific ideal of mobility and adaptability under the rhetoric of free trade, according to which a "bad" citizen is one who is lazy and inflexible, or who fails to balance his/her life choices properly and becomes a burden on others. Socially dysfunctional drug addicts, for example, are contemptible not because taking drugs is totally unacceptable (freedom to seek pleasure is one of neoliberal culture's core ideals), but because they cannot then fulfil all the demands of self-sufficiency. In a way, addiction of any kind indicates that an individual is following *one of* neoliberalism's demands to the letter: the shopaholic is obsessed with acquiring new goods, the workaholic with career advancement and so on. Yet they still fail because according to its impossible expectations we are supposed to do *everything* to this same extreme level all at once.

This concept of freedom also extends to issues of government, around a central principle of democracy that functions as a sort of consumer choice. In the political landscape, notions of citizenship, the nation, community or religion are still part of the discourse, and sometimes even clash with free trade ideals. However, actual political policy in recent decades has been largely a matter of pragmatic management based on the ability of a government to run the country as a business, with the general aim being to help the market system run smoothly through institutional support and a focus on deregulation, privatization and reduced public services. For the voter, democracy then becomes a matter of selecting the mainstream party that seems to best ensure economic stability, or to represent the most likely source of personal financial gain. In other words, the democratic process is packaged as an opportunity to select the brand that best accords with one's lifestyle, identity and interests, rather than a way of determining the workings of society. There is no room on the table to consider problems with capitalism itself, or properly discuss concepts such as market regulation, the organization of work and the social effects of rampant consumerism. We are merely asked to give our stamp of approval for the way things are at infrequent intervals (while also being fully responsible if things go wrong).

Moreover, the accompanying connotation of this politics is that the state should never actively try to steer social development, as that would oppose "freedom" by calling for a centralized control that curtails choice and undermines efficiency. Indeed, a major tenet of neoliberal ideology is that planned economies are doomed to failure, in part because people themselves are inherently flawed. Simply put, if we try to plan and organize how social development happens, we will be the victims of our own hubris and fall into totalitarianism, so to save ourselves from ourselves, the only workable option is the "neutral" non-human balancing mechanism of the market. Interesting here is that, as much as neoliberalism optimistically celebrates the potential of each individual human to realize his/her own fulfilment, it pessimistically dismisses any attempt to combine that potential in collective endeavour. In this way, neoliberal ideology effectively includes its own get-out clause, as it does not matter if the existing capitalist society has problems and doesn't work anything like as smoothly as it is supposed to. It only matters that anything else would be worse because it would create lower overall standards of living and restrict our freedom to choose. In some ways, this is a perfectly rational and realistic idea, exemplified by historical ruins such as that of the Soviet Union. But the scare stories about failed utopias are also ideological tools that serve to block proper consideration of major alterations to the market system that may be required, or obscure how the market is inherently unable to fulfil its promises because its impersonal logic doesn't always accord with our social needs.

If these are the core "contents" of neoliberal ideology, we should also explore the "form" it takes, or how it actually functions as the background to modern life. To an extent it can be understood through Karl Marx's concept of ideology as a set of ruling ideas, in that: "The class which has the means of material production at its disposal, consequently also controls the means of mental production, so that the ideas of those who lack the means of mental production are on the whole subject to it." In this way, Marx continues, the members of the ruling class "regulate the production and distribution of the ideas of their age."[6] Yet we can add to this that the neoliberal background ideology also comprises various assumptions embodied in and reproduced through the institutional structures of society, which effectively condition behaviour. While it is still the case that the economic interests of an influential elite are cemented in this process, it does not necessarily mean that this group consciously promotes neoliberalism as some grand social project, and may themselves merely follow their personal ambitions (defined in part by neoliberal ideals), or fulfil designated roles within the organizations they work for. Similarly, the less wealthy majority may not be under the influence of specific dominant ideas so much as simply trying to survive and succeed, which involves working in accordance with neoliberal demands. At the most basic level, most of us experience an immediate need to earn money to pay bills and live comfortably, and there is again something very rational and realistic in perceiving normal work-leisure routines as essential to a good life, based on building stable foundations around a career, a home, a family and some disposable income. Given the lack of existing alternatives, not entering this cycle seems objectively worse, whether or not people consciously believe in the veracity or morality of neoliberal ideals.

At the same time, I do not want to suggest by mentioning these "structural" functions of neoliberal ideology that what people believe is no longer significant. There is certainly a degree to which people across the social spectrum reproduce current systems purely through their behaviour, even when they criticize these systems outwardly or simply do not think about them, as they focus solely on the everyday tasks in front of them. In fact, this kind of rationality, in which we deal with what is rather than what could be, is especially compatible with that neoliberal logic that interprets everything as a calculable value. It means we are left constantly managing ways to maximize our incomes and weighing that effort against our overall "work-life balance," rather than wondering whether the circumstances and aims themselves are problematic. Such rationality may even seem to replace any actual ideology we might have, because the constant evaluations we make to decide which actions are most beneficial tend to override consistent philosophies or value systems. Such thinking is defined by Jürgen Habermas as "technocratic consciousness," which he also describes as a "glassy background ideology" whose scientific rationality replaces traditional ideological belief to a large extent.[7] But I do not see this mode of thinking as the whole story, as it doesn't fully explain people's acceptance of the existing social order, especially if their best efforts do not result in satisfaction. As we have seen, neoliberal ideology involves notions of what should make us happy. These ideas must then themselves indicate a set of social and personal goals, even ethical ideals, which frame a great deal of people's justifications for their behaviour. In essence, "technocratic consciousness" is supplemented by something more recognizably "ideological" that *rationalizes* the focus on what is rather than what could be. Even if we simply follow our immediate economic needs we can explain *why* that seems like the best thing to do, and it still matters what we believe and what we desire.

This point is important as I consider ideology not only as a social background of assumptions and pressures, but also in terms of different ways in which people justify behaving in accordance with that background. And this is important in neoliberal capitalism especially because, although it makes demands upon us, those demands do not simply programme us to fulfil specific social roles but encourage us to make choices and take responsibility for them. The inevitable result of this open-ended demand, more than with more traditional forms of ideology, is a variety of interpretations, and these interpretations are ideological in that they revolve around different beliefs, values and conditions according to which they accept the existing social order. As already mentioned, neoliberalism pulls us in different directions at once with its multifaceted and often mutually incompatible concepts of fulfilment. On one hand we are supposed to feel guilty if we are not virtual workaholics, because any failure to meet constant career targets is a sign we don't work hard enough. On the other hand we are encouraged to binge watch box sets of "must see" TV shows and lead busy social lives, as well as go to the gym and spend "quality time" with our spouses and children, all of course while getting plenty of sleep, eating well and avoiding stress. In effect, the neoliberal demand may be summed up in the oxymoronic slogan found in UK alcoholic drinks advertising: "enjoy responsibly." Because of the way the demand is framed we cannot satisfy either side of it; there is always more enjoyment to be had, but too much makes us irresponsible, while being too responsible means failing to enjoy enough. Perhaps in earlier forms of consumer capitalism a balance was possible, as expectations of work and downtime were not overinflated by the sense that we must maximize every potential. Now we are supposed to ceaselessly strive for the limit in every area of life, and there is no concrete way to reconcile this impossible demand. It is hardly surprising if beliefs about what is right and what is a good life have become less uniform than ever before.

To a degree, neoliberalism itself has answers to the difficult questions it poses, as it factors in the contradictions people experience, and reinterprets these as human failures to properly implement or realize neoliberal ideas. According to this logic, it's not the system that fails us, but we who fail the system, by cheating, shirking responsibility or making irrational choices. Or, the freedoms offered by neoliberalism are not made fully available because government bureaucracy still regulates the economy too much. In this way, the neoliberal fantasy not only tells us what to desire but also what stops us from getting it, so when it inevitably falls short of its promises that failure is already excused. As Slavoj Žižek explains through the psychoanalytic concepts of Jacques Lacan, this double-sided unconscious fantasy is part of all ideology, and creates a circuit of self-affirmation that is very difficult to break because it takes its own failure into account in advance. In neoliberalism's case, because any particular person *can* succeed it is our own fault if we don't, or the fault of someone else who exploited the system in a way that wasn't intended. These notions obscure how the system's emphasis on competitive individualism itself encourages us to find exploits and shortcuts that often have detrimental effects on others, or that there simply isn't enough room at the top for everyone to win, even if we each have some hope of "making it" at the individual level.

But what happens when even these inbuilt defence mechanisms can't quite cover the range and scope of contradictions that people experience? For example, the exhortation to maximize our potential in all areas of life sets an extremely high bar. Advertising and celebrity culture expose us to images of successful and fulfilling lifestyles that we have no realistic hope of reaching, or which don't actually exist. Meanwhile, the opportunities to enjoy high quality education, career choice, ownership of property and consumer luxuries are simply far more accessible to some than others. For those without money, connections or "marketable" personal qualities, the formal freedom to "make it big" is thus near meaningless, and the idea that we are all personally responsible for our success inadequate. Even the supposed agency of democracy is ineffectual here, when major parties have unified around reducing state services, rather than expanding them to enable more equal access to opportunities in practice, so there is rarely a mainstream political option to reverse that trend. This loss of "big government," so central to neoliberalism, may be experienced as problematic in other ways as well, simply because a society based on individual competition inevitably produces losers. That is, even if extreme private wealth does in some way create the proverbial rising tide that lifts all boats, it doesn't help the many people who were thrown overboard to make it rise. State support is still required for these supposed "failures" (from the long-term unemployed and victims of market crashes to those who suffer from addictions, or anxiety, depression and other conditions), if they are not to clog the wheels of "freedom." And it is particularly hard to reconcile the loss of welfare services when the inefficient state bureaucracy neoliberalism claims to eradicate re-emerges in private transactions. In today's world, everything from productivity to healthcare to leisure is monitored and recorded through inflated bureaucratic procedures, whether performance assessments at work, sales contracts peppered with complex clauses, or customer service interactions and surveys designed to gather our information or extract more money. The important point here is that such bureaucracy is not a glitch in the otherwise smooth flow of neoliberal processes, but intrinsic to how modern companies remain competitive and increase profits. The sense that neoliberalism's "freedom" is actually very invasive to our privacy is hard to shift.

Perhaps the most overwhelming obstacle to our acceptance of neoliberal conditions, however, is that sense of bewilderment caused by the contrasting nature of social demands and the onus on personal responsibility. Simply put, it is difficult to know which guidelines to follow, what to prioritize or where the acceptable boundaries of behaviour lie. Without the apparent clarity of meaning and official moral standards imposed by more outwardly dogmatic social systems, individuals may feel that they have *too much* responsibility to decide the course of their lives. As Beck's notion of the risk regime suggests, the risk of free choice is placed on individuals who are increasingly atomized and increasingly vulnerable within shifting economic circumstances, whose rules are often too complex or vague to understand. We often don't know which decisions are correct until we have seen the results, by which time it may be difficult to undo any damage to our careers, bank balances, relationships or health. For sure, there is no shortage of advice, as we are bombarded with information from all kinds of public and private media sources, but we may well end up with directly contradictory ideas whose deeper agendas can be hard to identify. Often, it is not even clear whether our "self-interest" should be strictly narrow and focused on our immediate desires or involve ethical responsibilities towards society. The very fact that so-called ethical consumerism (Fairtrade, organic produce) is *only* an individual consumer decision, for example, sends mixed messages about its importance. Alternatively, it may be that our socially motivated choices, such as responsible purchases and voting decisions, begin to appear fruitless, while reinventing our identities and styles doesn't make us feel happier after all. Consequently, it may become difficult to believe that any of the choices provided as neoliberal freedoms are really meaningful.

Despite these very plausible reactions to modern social conditions, people for the most part continue to do what they are supposed to. To reiterate, I see this "conformism" as involving various supplementary ideological fantasies and rationalizations, beyond simple capitulation to immediate economic necessity. So *how* do people reconcile these contradictions with their life goals and daily experience? Following the Lacanian model of ideology developed by Žižek and others, we can see this relationship as one in which each individual has an *unconscious* "fantasy" that organizes his/her desire, creating a sense of what should be fulfilling as well as what blocks that fulfilment. This fantasy then enables a kind of deep, undefined acceptance of the way things are without necessarily entailing conscious subscription to the ideals of neoliberalism and free trade. But, as I see it, these unconscious fantasies are still supported by certain conscious beliefs and rationalizations, or the things we tell ourselves to justify acting in accordance with neoliberal demands even when we see their flaws. It is here that neoliberalism functions as the invisible background, in that accepting its demands still requires internalization of some of its deeper assumptions (including, when all else fails, its trump card: "there is no alternative"), and not looking at social problems as the result of neoliberalism itself. Rationalization is then effectively a way of making sense of neoliberal demands when they don't make sense on their own terms, in a way that ultimately reaffirms the base concepts provided by neoliberalism itself.

In this book I consider four such responses to neoliberal demands, which I identify as hedonism, cynical self-interest, escapist defeatism and reformism. In this schema, hedonism is a kind of belief in fulfilment through consumer pleasures, cynical self-interest is an individualized attempt to thrive within a flawed, corrupt system, escapist defeatism is an obsessive fixation on fictional entertainment to escape alienation and uncertainty, and reformism is a belief in the possibility of correcting flaws in the fundamentally acceptable structures of the system. Each of these responses can be seen as having a belief system of sorts. In the cases of reformism and even hedonism, there remain notions of a social ideal that follows neoliberal ideas but wishes for changes to be made, based on certain values or concepts of meaning. For instance, individuals may think that things would be fine "if only people adhered to stricter ethical codes," or "if only politicians did more to eradicate corruption," or, from a hedonistic view, "if only we learned to live and let live," or "if only people simply relaxed and enjoyed life's pleasures." Conversely, cynical or defeatist individuals may recognize that the system is more fundamentally broken but still accept it, perhaps because it is too difficult to change or because it is not worth the effort and risk, especially when they are in relatively privileged positions themselves. As I aim to show, however, even these responses contain underlying beliefs in facets of the background ideology, such as in their valorization of individual effort, responsibility and self-expression, or in their pessimistic accounts of human nature.

At the same time, and as I define these positions in detail through different videogames, I consider that they relate to neoliberal demands in ambiguous ways, internalizing background assumptions *and* registering a sense of dissatisfaction. The games represent dysfunctional modern societies and feature characters who struggle against antagonisms within them. In doing so, they transcend everyday agency to resist authority in some way, but never fully escape neoliberal expectations. Both the narratives and systems of play in these games therefore tend to reinforce existing ideals rather than fully evaluate and criticize them—the power fantasies fail to confront the social problems they identify at the root. Yet, although they do not interrogate neoliberal ideology itself, they at least demand something that neoliberal society fails to provide. There is a kind of unformulated depiction of deeper contradictions in their form of expression, not as actual ideologies with a specific political programme, but as cultural objects. As games and power fantasies, they imply a dissatisfaction with reality *and* the perceived impossibility of actually resolving it, hence the need for the imaginary resolution. We are still left with the unanswered question of what is so unfathomable and so insurmountable in reality that it can only be represented as a fiction, but the representation itself points to the existence of that real problem, as something we must try to express and confront. Similarly, I feel that the everyday instances of the ideological responses to neoliberalism that the games represent contain the same ambiguity, being simultaneously connected to neoliberalism and dissatisfied with it, leaving a space for alternative ideas to develop.

3

Saints Row IV: The City as Playground

Saints Row is a series of open-world "sandbox" games set predominantly in modern urban environments. This means that, although there are distinct, story-driven "missions" to complete in a specific order, in between these players can move freely around the city and partake of its various interactive elements without the pressure of pre-defined objectives. Narratively, the series revolves around the criminal exploits of the Saints, a street gang which grows in stature and renown with each instalment. The player controls a character simply known as "the boss," with the other gang members acting as computer-controlled backup and various forms of tactical support. By the third game in the series, *Saints Row: The Third* (*SRIII*), and even more so in *Saints Row IV* (*SRIV*), the Saints have transcended their original status to become an internationally recognized brand. And as the scope widens, the tone becomes less serious and more outlandish. The characters in *SRIV* are cartoonish pleasure-seekers, the humour is crude and self-deprecating, and the player experience prioritizes mindless destructive fun over the challenge or strategic depth found in many other games. The story serves to place the gang in increasingly ludicrous and spectacular situations, creating scenes that resemble explosive action movies and poke fun at pop culture, into which the Saints excitedly throw themselves with no concern for the consequences. As players, we charge around the cityscape, stumbling into numerous brief distractions based on racing, fighting, shooting and blowing things up, with a constant stream of overpowered weapons and vehicles encouraging the havoc. The result is an entertaining violent hedonism that is both framed as fulfilling in itself and rewarded by progress in the game.

Where *SRIV* takes the formula a step further from its predecessors is in replacing its own "real-world" setting in the game with a virtual reality. Through a plot device involving an alien invasion, the *SRIII*'s fictional city of Steelport is recreated as a computer simulation, allowing the game to completely disconnect its entertaining distractions from any last pretence of real-life limitation. What is important ideologically here is that this shift between *SRIII* and *SRIV* signifies more than the obvious escalation in scale and absurdity. That is, the detachment of the power fantasy from reality appears as an unconscious attempt to resolve contradictions that plagued the real-world setting. While *SRIV* remains a hedonistic fantasy, it attempts to present a far more utopian hedonism that sheds the sense of exploitation prevalent in the previous game. In particular, it removes the link between consumer pleasures and money, so now the Saints can enjoy near-unfettered access to their destructive desires without leaving behind a trail of undeserving victims. But what does not change is the content of these desires, which are still very much informed by individualistic consumerist ideals of enjoyment. Its effective aim is to present the ultimate "frictionless" consumer fantasy, outside the world itself. Yet because it escapes reality to realize this dream it never actually names or confronts the antagonism between consumer pleasure and exploitation, and instead merely sidesteps the issue. The neoliberal concept of consumer pleasure as fulfilment remains the background foundation, and as such the sense of rebellion, with all its violence and law breaking, comes to feel sanitized and mundane. Indeed, *SRIV* effectively reconstructs its hedonism as an anti-authoritarian force for good, in line with the neoliberal fantasy of free trade.

SRIV represents consumerist hedonism in the sense that its content and cultural references reflect the presumed desires of a thrill-seeking, male youth: fast cars, strippers, raucous music, video games, action films and guns. But while it therefore reflects one part of the (neoliberal) American dream, the trappings of success, it rejects any ideal of earning that success through hard work. If, as mentioned in the last chapter, the dominant demand of neoliberalism is "enjoy responsibly," *SRIV*'s characters take the "enjoy" part very seriously while dismissing the "responsibly" part completely. Perhaps such a response is an inevitable danger in a social climate that asks not for everything in moderation but for everything to be maximized—neoliberalism really does ask us to fully indulge our desire for pleasure, albeit at the same time it asks us to satisfy other, conflicting desires to an equally endless degree. So what if we feel that trying to really fulfil one aspect of the neoliberal demand is a more authentic response than only partially fulfilling all the aspects? What if the demand for continuous toil to afford our pleasures seems irrational when the pleasures themselves are supposed to require all our time and attention? Is it possible, as philosopher and critical theorist Herbert Marcuse theorized decades ago, that the promises of consumerism may provoke desires that transcend the products themselves, and cannot be satisfied within the capitalist reality? The majority of us may still subscribe to balance, but in everyday life we can see those who have been drawn into this alternative approach, such as addicts (not only drug addicts, but sex addicts, shopaholics and so on) or those obsessed with celebrity culture and its associated dreams of fame and fortune. *SRIV* embodies this condition, with a sense of fun that seemingly obeys the demand for pleasure to the exclusion of all other demands.

Staying with Marcuse, he also considered whether this dissatisfaction created by capitalism may foster "transcendent" needs according to which people begin to reconsider what is socially important, even beyond capitalism itself, or whether it remains formulated on narrow libidinal enjoyment of sexual and violent pleasures. In *SRIV*, the former possibility is never considered, as the desires it embodies continue to be framed by consumer entertainment. Its ideology is one that has deeply absorbed these pleasures as measures of fulfilment, or swallowed the messages of pop culture, including films, TV, music, advertising and mainstream politics, whole. We are all familiar with the modern environment in which we are bombarded from an early age with a range of mediatized personality types and materialistic aspirations. And to an extent it is still the case even today that consumer demands "have created a second nature of man which ties him libidinally and aggressively to the commodity form."[8] In other words, the desire to obtain consumer goods of all kinds may be experienced by some as a "need," and is so entrenched that these individuals don't question or reflect upon it. *SRIV* encapsulates this notion of consumerist fulfilment as "second nature," as its critical scope never exceeds the sphere of pop culture or conceives alternative desires, even when the economic structure of capitalism is no longer present.

The problem *SRIV* implicitly tackles is then not that of how consumer desires are systematically provoked or reinforced, but the tension between obsession with consumer desires and how those desires are actually funded in the real world. This tension exists as an unresolved undercurrent in *SRIII*, where fun is conditional on money and hedonism involves the exploitation of others. In effect, *SRIII* manifests a blinkered, selfish hedonism, which simply associates fulfilment with pleasure so that happiness becomes a matter of the individual experiencing as much pleasure as possible. Drawing on Marcuse again, we can see this hedonistic philosophy as one that never questions what constitutes pleasure or why certain things are deemed especially pleasurable, and focuses purely on gratifying any desires that arise, using whatever means are available in the existing society. Such hedonism rejects unsatisfying labour, but does not imagine any ideal society which attempts to overcome social antagonisms or the need for labour. It has no utopian element as it lives completely in the moment, distorting into an extreme self-interest and competitiveness that treats others as mere instruments. In *SRIII*, this limit is especially clear in its depictions of female sex workers. In one mission, the player is tasked with saving a group of prostitutes from sex traffickers, but after completing the mission must choose whether to sell the women on for a quick cash injection or force them to work as prostitutes for the Saints to provide a more long-term cash flow. According to the brand of hedonism promoted in the game, these options make sense simply because more money equals more opportunity for pleasure, even though it reduces the women to commodities. In *SRIII*, the female body is an object of enjoyment that is also exploitable for profit, and is thus forced to labour for the hedonist's pleasure.

Subsequently, despite never explicitly recognizing this particular tension, *SRIV* seems unable to stomach it anymore, and no longer seems fully satisfied with hedonism for its own sake. Thus, in a single destructive act it severs fun and freedom from their connection to money and (other people's) labour. In its utopian power fantasy, consumerist, hedonistic pleasure retains a central meaning and purpose, but *without* the exploitation. However, the only way it can realize this ideal is by exiting reality itself. The game's narrative begins with the boss of the Saints becoming President of the United States (and achieving results with a no-nonsense, politically incorrect approach). Yet, soon after, aliens invade and kidnap the Saints, imprisoning the boss in a sanitized computer simulation of Steelport. He/she (the player chooses the boss's gender and appearance) disrupts the simulation and escapes to an alien space craft that's been commandeered by another escaped Saint, Kinzie. The alien ruler reacts to this defiance by blowing up the whole world, after which the boss seeks revenge by re-entering the simulation and causing havoc, to reveal the locations of the other Saints and finally the alien ruler. In this way, the simulation city becomes the setting for the bulk of the game and, given that the aim is to cause disruption to progress, a prime location for unfettered and non-exploitative destructive entertainment. Thus the perfect hedonistic utopia is created, and all it costs to realize it is the world. In effect, *SRIV* embodies Jameson's oft-quoted point that, "It seems to be easier for us today to imagine the thoroughgoing deterioration of the earth and of nature than the breakdown of late capitalism."[9] That is, *SRIV* cannot posit an alternative form of fulfilment, or a social formation that could support it, only a choice between the continuation of capitalist antagonisms and a shift outside reality into a virtual world. It implies some vague notion that there is something dysfunctional about consumerist desire in capitalist societies, that something should change, and even that a unifying cause (fighting the aliens) may be necessary. But it doesn't identify the problem as such, or recognize that consumerist desire itself could be questioned.

The change to a virtual reality setting in *SRIV* produces a number of repercussions in terms of how the player interacts with the game and the "rhetoric" that is produced. First, although in practice the simulation retains a basic "economy" to encourage player exploration and regulate advancement (players can purchase abilities and upgrades after successfully completing certain tasks or collecting items), many of the main pleasures it offers are free. Most notably, the boss's avatar within the simulation has superhuman abilities, allowing him/her to run at great speeds, rapidly scale buildings, freeze enemies with ice and so on. With this increased freedom of movement and destructive power, the vehicles that were previously a big part of the series are rendered almost redundant, even a less entertaining mode of travel, but can easily be materialized at will if the player so wishes. Various weapons, meanwhile, are offered as rewards for fulfilling objectives, bought for next to nothing at virtual shops, or merely picked up from defeated foes.

Overall, therefore, despite the pre-defined missions that lead to the game's ending, the core power fantasy in *SRIV* is one of free rein in the city: traversing the landscape in great bounds, causing joyful mayhem with near impunity (squads of alien goons try to stop you, but are rarely cause for concern), and constantly switching from one entertaining distraction to the next. One minute you're climbing a huge tower, the next you're gunning down waves of aliens, or racing through the streets, or brawling in an arena, or getting deliberately hit by traffic to see how long you can remain airborne. It's a relentless parade of short attention span diversions, which are fun and funny in their exaggerated execution. *SRIV's* 3D space is thus a playground or assault course. While this kind of "open world" in videogames is always to some degree merely a structure that links objectives together or provides arenas for play, as opposed to a believable functioning environment, in *SRIV* the city is only that; its buildings are not workplaces or homes, even superficially, they are purely shapes that are entertaining to traverse. And of course, since the world is not real even within the game's fiction, both the character's avatar and NPCs in the simulation can be (ab)used without consequence. Careless and reckless behaviour is encouraged, as no real harm can come to the boss and "collateral damage" is meaningless.

The question may be asked how this hedonistic utopia could still be deemed consumerist, as its activities are not really commodified. The answer here is in noting the continuity from *SRIII* in terms of what is deemed valuable, and the way freedom is viewed from the consumerist perspective of fulfilment through individualistic pleasure. In *SRIV*, individual identity is still expressed through our choice of goods, such as weaponry, vehicles and outfits, and the boss stands out from the rest of the simulation precisely due to having *exclusive* access to the most impressive examples. Meanwhile, the game's many references to other media are confined to mainstream film, music and videogames, similarly reinforcing the boundaries of desire around popular commodified culture. The "second nature" of consumerism remains. The result, in one sense, is inclusive and multiculturalist—the gang comprises different genders, races, nationalities and classes, all of which freely express their identities. Yet we can't forget that this freedom is not universal freedom, because most of the world's population have been sacrificed to realize it, and because it remains restricted to choices of style, hobbies and sexual activity. In *SRIV*, as in consumer culture, individuality is constructed from a series of "off the peg" preferences, whose presence obscures the possibility of considering any more meaningful choices.

In this way, what *SRIV* lacks as a *utopian* fantasy is that its characters only consider how to get what they want, not how those wants are structured by particular social circumstances or how they might be intrinsically problematic. In short, to quote Marcuse again, its hedonism cannot "distinguish between true and false wants and interests and between true and false enjoyment. It accepts the wants and interests of individuals as simply given and as valuable in themselves."[10] What is "true" here is not that some wants are indisputably right and better than others, but that we should at least understand that the individualistic wants prescribed to us by social norms are not set in stone, and are "false" in the sense that they often appear unquestionable. Yet Marcuse also notes that hedonism has a more radical, emancipatory potential, because of the way it at least refuses dissatisfaction and maintains a demand for happiness. It follows that contained in this base refusal is some unformulated notion of a greater *social* realization of happiness, because if happiness is the aim then a social organization more conducive to *general* happiness, rather than the happiness of certain individuals, is desirable. *SRIV's* attitude goes as far as undermining the neoliberal demand for self-actualization through work, as well as exploding the relationship between enjoyment and capital. By taking the promises of consumer pleasure seriously, it demonstrates that the freedom associated with consumer choice clashes with other social expectations, and hints at an antagonism between the demand to enjoy ourselves and the demands of labour. However, because *SRIV* does not confront or even consciously recognize this antagonism, and merely tries to erase rather than actually resolve it, there is no wider concept of liberty within its world. Unable to see and analyse the neoliberal background explicitly, its implicit social critique cannot yet represent the deeper utopian core of hedonism.

The other point about *SRIV*'s rules and objectives, and the way they actively encourage destruction and havoc, is that procedurally and aesthetically they present irresponsible, violent pleasure-seeking as *the* means to overcome social antagonism. In this way, the Saints' violence is no longer the immoral criminal activity of gangland turf wars, but the manifestation of hedonism as a *moral* response to the alien invasion. Liberated from the "purity" of enjoyment for its own sake and the total self-interest that comes with it in *SRIII*, the hedonism in *SRIV* rationalizes itself according to a bigger, ethical cause. But, in doing so, its implied politics of free expression falls back onto clear neoliberal tropes, even as it does away with the capitalist system. If the underlying tension in *SRIII* was the contradictory effect (pleasure and exploitation) of individualistic consumer capitalism, in *SRIV* it emerges in the Saints' confrontation with the authoritarian aliens, who clearly embody a "big government" that tries to block our personal freedoms. These aliens perfectly represent the oppressive judgement, uniformity and regulation so regularly demonized by free-market neoliberals. The alien ruler is a totalitarian dictator, overseeing a strict bureaucratic order and attempting to restrict enjoyment. When the boss is first trapped in the simulation, it takes the form of a 1950s style sitcom, in which everybody is supposed to play pre-defined roles and follow the script. Within the alien spacecraft, we hear announcements over its address system, which resemble exactly the kind of inane "health and safety" warnings we would expect from overbearing institutions on Earth. *SRIV*'s answer to this oppressive order is a cultural rebellion of violence, sexual freedom, loud music and absurd fashions. As Kinzie informs the boss, "The simulation is all about normalcy. Pleasantry. Order. All the things you hate...Go forth. Unleash hell." The great fear behind *SRIV*'s power fantasy is that of losing consumer freedoms to a collectively organized or socialist society.

To take this point further, as the boss has become the President of the USA, he/she *is* America, reacting against this very "un-American" threat to the pluralist-consumerist American dream. Certainly, any flag-waving patriotism in the game is very much tongue-in-cheek, but it is still the case that, in the end, the Saints owe their rise to American culture and values, which must therefore be protected from an outside threat. The ideological result is a kind of youthful naivety, whose reasoning seems to earnestly mimic the kind of advertisement where conformism and uniformity are disrupted by an "individual" who uses a certain hair product or brand of jeans to stand out. In some way, it presumably aims to channel the spirit of cultural upheavals from the 1950s and 1960s with the idea that the powers that be can be "shocked" into submission by free expressions of style, sexual liberation, strong language and violent imagery. To maintain its delusions of efficacy, this kind of hedonism imagines an authority (a political elite) that is still outraged by such behaviour, to give its acting out meaning. Yet, of course, in reality such "rebellion" has long been a part of mainstream entertainment media, including *SRIV* itself, as a mass-produced cultural commodity. There is even a sense when playing *Saints Row* games that the more extreme, edgy and outlandish they try to be, the more mass market their appeal becomes.[11] The violence and destruction in *SRIV* that disrupts the aliens so much is thus in line with the demands of neoliberalized consumer society, and the Saints' sense of rebellion doesn't extend to challenging any actually existing social order. The message at the heart of *SRIV*'s hedonism is still a robust defence of American individualism, and a call to protect and reinstate a neoliberal order to maintain consumer freedoms.

Finally, while *SRIV* therefore has a kind of political *position*, it has no political *programme*, and indeed the hedonistic utopia it creates and celebrates with its simulated city is ultimately destroyed by the very behaviour it promotes. By the end of the game, the simulation is corrupted and worthless, and the Earth is still gone. All that survives are the Saints, a handful of other humans, the alien spaceships and many of the low-level alien soldiers. The boss kills the alien ruler and takes his throne, leading the remaining aliens to accept the boss as their new ruler, and put their technological prowess at the Saints' disposal. So it seems that a select group of humans can now go on to start a new world. But have we not then come full circle, as the aliens become the source of exploitable labour that will serve the desires of the human elite in presumably building and maintaining a more permanent hedonistic utopia? Again, the social order will rest on hierarchical division, where free expression is for the few, maintained by the enslavement of the many. Because the antagonism has not been resolved it returns, and the Saints remain oblivious to it. On one hand, then, the utopian playground city couldn't sustain the presence of the Saints' chaotic ultra-freedom, which tears down the state and with it the whole platform that facilitates their behaviour. It seems that, although consumerist enjoyment always falls short when combined with responsibility, because we can never dedicate ourselves enough to it, without that tempering responsibility the unfettered pursuit of consumerist fulfilment becomes an explosion of libidinal aggression that destroys its own foundations. On the other hand, the only way to rebuild a more lasting environment for consumerist desire is to take the responsibility to organize a new institutional base, which also requires a new exploitable labour force to construct it, unless the work and the pleasure were distributed equally. The irony is that the very thing individualistic hedonism rails against — a network of social institutions that controls and oppresses the majority — is precisely what keeps it alive.

4

Grand Theft Auto V: The City as Battleground

Grand Theft Auto is one of the biggest franchises in gaming, and pioneer of the urban, open-world, sand box genre, from whose roots games such as *Saints Row* have grown. It is also one of the most widely discussed game series in both mainstream media and academia.[12] *Grand Theft Auto V* (*GTAV*), the most recent instalment to date, repeats the formula established in previous titles while elevating it to an unprecedented scale, with a sprawling and detailed environment based on Los Angeles and its surrounding areas, and an intertwining narrative which switches player control between three different characters. As always in *Grand Theft Auto* games, the characters are career criminals and game objectives tend to revolve around stealing and driving various vehicles, but also incorporate shoot-outs and other distractions. In a sense, the potential for undirected play and irresponsible, destructive fun in *GTAV* is similar to that of *SRIV*, yet its city environment is more detailed and realistic, its narrative strands more complex, and its comic tone more world-weary and satirical. Most importantly, for our purposes, its main ideological thrust that of an unwavering cynicism towards modern life.

The cynical attitude in *GTAV* seems to emerge from a high level of social awareness combined with a bottomless pessimism. So, although it is the only game among the four analyzed in this book that explicitly identifies capitalism as a major source of social dysfunction, it also holds out no hope for progressive change. Both in the game's narrative and its mission structures, rewards and distractions, it reproduces a consumer capitalist cycle of work, financial accumulation and leisure time, and imagines no alternative. In this way, its critique of capitalism is really quite superficial, and the power fantasy it offers is actually one of "making it" within existing conditions. It never endorses any outward belief in the ethical arguments for dominant neoliberal demands, but shows us how to win by obeying them anyway, or how to be part of the elite in a dog-eat-dog world, rather than one of its exploited dupes. Despite their cynicism, then, and even the criminal nature of their activities, the characters in *GTAV* are in a sense the perfect capitalist subjects. They find their satisfaction in the power fantasy of entrepreneurial capital accumulation, even as they distance themselves from it, and will do anything to achieve success. The ethics of what they do is hardly important, since everyone in the world of *GTAV* is corrupt; all that matters is their ability to balance work and enjoyment, which they manage admirably.

The kind of cynicism promoted in *GTAV* is well established in theories of ideology. As already mentioned, in essence it is a kind of socially aware pessimism, according to which the existing society is hopelessly corrupt, but cannot surmount that corruption because it is too deeply embedded, if not at the core of human nature itself. Cynics thus see hypocrisy and ulterior motives in all official values and moralistic claims, and consider dishonesty and self-interest to be universal conditions, so there is no "sincere" alternative ideal that could assume control instead. This is a philosophy largely summed up in the phrase "if you can't beat 'em, join 'em," as the only realistic choice it perceives is to either exploit the system's corruption to one's advantage, or mindlessly obey its fake moral standards and be exploited. In social theory, a well-known formulation of this position is found in Peter Sloterdijk's concept of "cynical reason," or an unhappy "enlightened false consciousness," that he claims is diffuse in modern societies. As Sloterdijk explains it, cynics do not "understand their way of existing as something that has to do with being evil, but as participation in a collective, realistically attuned way of seeing things." This attitude leads to individualistic self-preservation, and cynics "know what they are doing, but they do it because...the force of circumstances and the instinct for self-preservation are speaking the same language, and they are telling them that it has to be so."[13] Larger social concerns are ignored as the individual prioritizes personal advancement, "knowing" that each of us must sink or swim, and that social improvement is impossible.

This concept of cynicism is further developed by Žižek, especially in terms of how, psychologically, subjects justify actions that apparently contradict their declared beliefs. On one hand, cynics' behaviour still effectively conforms to society's neoliberalized expectations, in the sense that they keep working and consuming according to the requirements of their narrow individual interests. The official moral values of neoliberalism may be empty, but for the cynic that is no reason to actually disrupt the structures of power that propagate them. On the other hand, cynics retain a moral position of their own, at least in theory, as they can appreciate that exploitation and manipulation are wrong, and claim to indulge in such activities only because they *have to*, since everyone else does it. As Žižek puts it, cynicism recognizes "the particular interest behind the ideological universality, the distance between the ideological mask and the reality, but it still finds reasons to retain the mask."[14] Yet at the same time, Žižek also points out how this "realistic" approach to modern life still misses something, which is how much cynics actually "enjoy" their apparently reluctant conformism, or how committed they are deep down to their actions. Put in psychoanalytical terms, they have an *unconscious* attachment which ties them to their behaviour, and get a libidinal satisfaction from it, while conscious "disavowal" is the means by which they avoid confrontation with that hidden truth. That is, their given reasons for acting contrary to their conscious moral beliefs, such as the universality of corruption or the lack of alternatives to the status quo, are how they rationalize and repress their internalization of neoliberal expectations.

Another point emphasized by Sloterdijk, Žižek and others is that this cynicism is especially dominant in modern societies. As Žižek says, "the prevailing ideology is that of cynicism; people no longer believe in ideological truth; they do not take ideological propositions seriously."[15] To the extent this is the case, we can see this widespread cynicism as a reaction to specific social conditions, and particularly from assumptions and beliefs that can be associated with neoliberalism. Specifically, the pessimism in cynical attitudes presupposes certain notions about human potential and social planning, especially the idea that, even if today's society is corrupt and dysfunctional, any change will only make it worse. In this way, it appears necessary to the supposedly detached, politically-neutral cynic to actively oppose any plan for radical change, based on a strong belief that attempts to make things better always go disastrously wrong. We can trace this idea to neoliberal notions about planned economies, and the example of the Soviet Union as a utopian dream that was inevitably thwarted by human flaws. Such understanding is part of what Jameson calls "market ideology," which "assures us that human beings make a mess of it when they try to control their destinies ('socialism is impossible') and that we are fortunate in possessing an interpersonal mechanism—the market—which can substitute for human hubris and planning and replace human decisions altogether."[16] Along these lines, the cynic does not see the neoliberal economic structure as ideal, and recognizes the damage its competitive individualism engenders, but still perceives that the market enables a level of balance that exceeds the potentials of human planning. To maintain this thinking, it is essential to retain a clear concept of human nature that emphasizes its greed and self-interest, as well as cautionary tales of planned societies, to challenge any proposals for social improvement.

So how does this mode of cynicism fit into *GTAV*? Put simply, the cynical view is personified in its three main characters, and then persistently vindicated through the events of the story and the other inhabitants in the game's city, Los Santos. The game's support cast in particular embodies the corruption and self-absorption that the cynic assumes is all pervasive. NPCs are often encountered in a state of mania, shouting demands at anyone who will listen, completely focused on their own immediate desires. Through this parade of entitled teens, hipster tech-entrepreneurs, backward hillbillies, exercise junkies, conceited celebrities, seedy paparazzi, greedy media producers, lazy drug addicts and shady dealers, littered throughout slums, suburbs and upmarket enclaves alike, *GTAV* portrays an anti-society. There are no institutional supports here, and people only tolerate others at all to the extent they appear useful. In essence, the demands of competitive individualism and aspirational consumerism have run amok, shaping people's desires in a way that leaves no space for altruism or sympathy. Either there never were any decent people, or they have long since succumbed to the harsh conditions. All that remains is an angry mass of monadic units, attempting to fulfil their unending want for money, fame, power or pleasure by any means.

What is crucial in terms of its ideology is that *GTAV* does not present this scenario as some dystopian nightmare, so much as just the way things are. Despite the comically exaggerated style of its situations and dialogue, the underlying implication is that they reflect our social "reality," as if finally this cutting satire removes the veil from modern life to reveal its ugly naked truth. The simple act of moving through the city, for example, is unavoidably aggressive and confrontational, creating a kind of all-against-all battlefield. More than other games, Los Santos appears as a convincing urban space, yet its inhabitants are never friendly and can be nothing more than service providers, competitors or victims. In particular, the primary mode of travel is to approach a stationary car, grab the driver from inside, throw them onto the road, then get in and drive away. *GTAV* does not shy away from criticizing the capitalist system and its false promises (indeed, the hyper-competitive individualism and lack of state presence beyond law enforcement that it depicts can be seen as a dark reflection of neoliberal ideals) nor even the human condition itself, for the absolute corruption of society. But at the same time, nothing in its world suggests there is anything remarkable or changeable about this situation.

The only alternative perspective in *GTAV*, and the one through which we observe its events, is thus the streetwise cynicism of its main characters, or at least the first two, Franklin and Michael, which functions as an oasis of rationality among the madness (the third character, Trevor, is himself something of an unstable psychopath, although still more socially aware than most). In effect, because they can see "clearly," these characters "know" that the madness around them is all there is, so they have no option but to function within it. Rational detachment does not excuse them from the battle, because it is universal, and even gives them a strategic advantage, as they are not blinded by narrow narcissistic pursuits. What seems to be missing for them, conversely, is a sense of meaning; while others buy into the consumerist American dream and become pathetic slaves to pleasure and money. Michael and Franklin's detached relationship to it provides no obvious purpose. As Michael, the jaded, middle-aged "Italianesque" gangster says of his relatively luxurious living conditions, "Maybe I'm here because I'm just an idiot, who thinks that imported palm trees are a good substitute for not really knowing what the fuck you're doing on this earth." There is no real satisfaction in the life he has made, including in his relationships with other people. Even Michael's family have succumbed to the madness: his wife is having a barely-concealed affair with her tennis coach, his daughter is spoilt and fame-obsessed, and his son a directionless pothead. The palm trees and the big house may simply serve as a kind of insulation from the world.

As such, when Michael meets Franklin, a young, low-level, African-American criminal, he initially advises him to give up on crime. As he puts it, "You work hard, screw over everybody that you love, hurt, rob, kill indiscriminately and maybe...just maybe, if you're lucky, you become a three bit gangster. It's bullshit. Go to college. Then you can rip people off and get paid for it. It's called capitalism." This is clearly a cynical attitude which focuses on taking the easiest and most profitable route, and prefers legal pursuits not because they are more ethical but because they are less risky. Yet ultimately both characters do return to crime, with a different kind of justification based on notions of authenticity and exceptionalism. That is, Michael and Franklin remain distinct from the masses and their petty addictions, and retain a sense of "honesty," because at least they are not hypocrites who use the law to feign legitimacy. As *GTAV* makes clear, the business world is full of immoral and corrupt individuals, hiding behind a wholesome, liberal image. For example, we see the billionaire owner of social media site "Lifeinvader," Jay Norris, introducing a new product in front of an adoring crowd. He announces to rapturous cheers that, "We have one of the youngest work forces in the world! An average age of only 14.4 years. That's not just impressive. It's revolutionary!" Somehow, the crowd doesn't see or doesn't care how reprehensible this is, perhaps because, as long as the corporation is a "real business" that delivers what they want, its image is unimpeachable. In contrast, then, the criminal in *GTAV* is a hero, even if his actions are also despicable, because at least he gets his hands dirty and doesn't pretend to be clean. This recurrent theme in *Grand Theft Auto* games is in fact their critical strength, in how they foreground the covert violence of "normal" social relations by revealing its resemblance to the more controversial criminal violence.

44

For the most part, however, the power fantasy in *GTAV* is about finding success within its world, or making the most of the capitalism that it apparently disdains, and as such it affirms the status quo in a number of ways. Tonally, for example, it projects a certain "cool" image through its satirical humour and countless significations of ironic detachment (in contrast to the more "cheesy" non-judgemental celebration of pop culture in *SRIV*), but there is always something familiar about its characters, dialogue and scenarios. If we look a little closer, we see that its façade is entirely constructed of recycled imagery from other cult media. Its characters and scenarios merely comprise an "intertextual" collage of cut and pasted stylistic appropriations from film and TV (*Heat, The Town, The Sopranos, Breaking Bad, Boyz n the Hood, The Fast and the Furious, South Park*), stitched together with a soundtrack of well-known (but not mainstream) licensed music. The result is a perfect exemplar of "postmodernism" in the way Jameson defines it as a "cultural logic" of late capitalism whose "constitutive features" include "a new depthlessness," based in "a whole new culture of the image or the simulacrum," and "a consequent weakening of historicity."[17] In accordance with this idea, the cultural fragments that comprise Los Santos really do lack depth, or any sense of interconnection or social context. Even the game's satirical social commentary is a mere image of itself, or a reproduction of a certain comedic style that becomes disconnected from any discernible political perspective.

The world of *GTAV* is then a "simulacrum" in that it is a copy of something which never existed in the form depicted by the game, precisely because the process of copying expunges the history and social environment that initially inspired the source material. In other words, *GTAV* presents us with something familiar that reminds us of actual events and people, but has a "de-politicizing" effect. Its depthless reality is summed up by a poster displayed in Franklin's bedroom, which resembles the red and blue "HOPE" poster of Obama. Here, the face on the poster is not a political figure at all, but that of a rapper within *GTAV*'s world, with his name, "MADD," written beneath. The picture is thus a purely stylistic recreation, in which the political meaning of the sign makes way for apolitical consumer entertainment, as hope is literally replaced with madness. And, as Jameson tells us, this process of changing realities into flattened images "does more than merely replicate the logic of late capitalism; it reinforces and intensifies it."[18] Most crucially, *GTAV*'s cut and paste appropriation functions in line with the neoliberal focus on individual responsibility for social problems because its depthless critique removes any sense of tension based on race, gender or class antagonism, and any dynamic of political conformism and opposition. Instead, it portrays a world in which capitalism brings out the bad in everybody, creating a bitter struggle in which nobody is more guilty or innocent than anyone else. There are no hierarchies of power to challenge, as in *GTAV*'s post-bailout world we are all equally corrupt and worthy of scorn.

Moreover, if we view the game in *its* social context, as a commodified product in a global mega-franchise, there is something in its attitude of "telling it like it is" that itself comes across as cynical and coldly corporate. Its seemingly disparate components, from pretensions to HBO-style narrative maturity and smart satire, to the visceral draw of its basic actions (driving, shooting) and consumerist pleasures (fast cars, fashions, music, casual sex and sporting activities), are linked by their presumed broad appeal among a young, male, media-savvy audience. Through this lens it is apparent that all the elements in the game are calculated to fall within the targeted players' comfort zones, and any social critique is not intended to present any kind of intellectual or ideological challenge. It is through this logic, for example, that we can understand *GTAV*'s internally contradictory representation of sex. On one hand, there are implicit denunciations of sexual manipulation and infidelity, obsessions with bodily image and cosmetic surgery and the media focus on sexualized imagery. On the other, the game constantly objectifies women as strippers and prostitutes,[19] and entices players with cheap titillation. Without any sense of a gender politics, the game presents sexual exploitation as "wrong" in some undefined sense, but also simply "how things are," so the player is free to disapprove of the seedier aspects of the media *and* enjoy their own sexual consumerism without guilt, as an unavoidable part of modern life. In this way, *GTAV*'s apparent critical edge really only touches on a whole range of hot issues, while avoiding any commitment or taking of sides that might alienate members of that core male audience.[20]

In terms of actually playing the game too, the power fantasy we enact is in the end very close to the neoliberal ideal. First, despite Michael's lamentations about his palm trees, the enjoyment of consumer pleasure still shines through in *GTAV*. For all the cynical satirical commentary, the game would barely be worth playing if not for the enjoyment of its myriad distractions. As a huge sandbox game, it is filled with all manner of easily accessible activities for its characters, including playing golf, tennis or darts, parachute jumping, visiting strip clubs, illegal street racing, or joy riding and high-speed pursuits with police. So, as much as *GTAV* distances itself from the "earnest" hedonism of *SRIV*, a good portion of our time in the game will likely be spent on these frivolous pursuits. Second, however, it is not only the consumerist side of the neoliberal demand that is embraced, as the game's structure in fact recreates a kind of work-leisure cycle. In the missions that advance the story and introduce new locations and support characters, players regularly receive tasks that look suspiciously like labour. In some cases, these are actual forms of "legitimate" work, from repossessing cars, to driving a taxi or tow truck. But even the criminal "jobs," including major heists, often reduce interaction to following a series of precise orders. Missions generally begin with instructions to walk or drive to a certain point, and continue with commands to steal a car, follow or chase another vehicle, shoot certain targets or place explosives in a specific place. In these endeavours, it is not uncommon to spend multiple minutes simply following a line on a GPS map, with deviation from the course resulting in failure. These sections then primarily serve as opportunities for lengthy dialogues between characters, stripping the player of agency to force attention on their cynical philosophizing (as mentioned earlier, the apparent apolitical "realism" of cynicism is actually often very committed to promoting its cause). What this means is that there is rarely scope to approach missions in different ways, even when the events that occur appear spontaneous, and the player is a slave to a narrative who must "earn" advancement through laborious activity.

Given the restrictive nature of these missions, the question for the characters, and in turn the player, might be: why bother with them at all? Since the consumer pleasures in the game world are enticing, not to mention quite freely available, and since Franklin, Michael and Trevor supposedly have no real attachment to their work, why not just relax? There is no real need for the characters to put in the work for material rewards,[21] yet, as they are written, they remain fixated on their "career" advancement. The only conclusion is that, when pushed through the story, the characters do their "jobs" not because there is no alternative, but because they really enjoy conforming to the capitalist work ethic. Even in comparison to *Grand Theft Auto IV*, for example, where the player is to an extent pressurized into doing missions through a narrative that places its immigrant main character in an "alien" environment with serious debt, there is little sense of urgency to *GTAV*'s prescribed tasks. Although Michael does return to crime after getting in debt to some shady characters, he effectively creates this trouble for himself, as if looking for a reason to return to "work." It thus feels that the characters work not even for the money (which Michael, at least, already had), but for that sense of self-actualization that neoliberalism valorizes.

In this way, *GTAV's* core message is that hard work is a reward in itself, in what it makes you. This message is reinforced by the way the game's power fantasy of "making it big" is not something freely given to the player, but one that must be earned through obedient labour in its missions. In this sense, the characters are the perfect neoliberal entrepreneurs, and retain a strong sense of commitment to existing economic systems, rather than merely accepting them. They are not exploiting others because they have to, and regardless of how much they criticize the existing situation, they really do believe in neoliberalism's individualist philosophy. Their cynicism does not signify lack of ideological belief, but the means through which they avoid confronting their fanatical attachment to the enjoyment of individualistic competition and the demand to enjoy responsibly. Despite their incisive grasp on reality, the player characters in *GTAV* are perhaps even more reliant on neoliberal capitalism than the crazed dupes they encounter.

In one of the game's possible endings, the three characters all survive and kill off their main antagonist, a wealthy businessman called Devin Weston. Before killing him, Michael reprimands Devin for his unethical business practices, especially his reliance on outsourcing and offshoring. Subsequently, with Devin gone, the trio decide what to do next and the following exchange occurs: Trevor: "Then we can get back to the kind of capitalism we practice." Franklin: "Shit, I don't know how much more better that is than Devin's kind." Michael: "Oh. Hypocrisy, Franklin. Civilization's greatest virtue." When it comes to it, they know that their own "kind of capitalism" is hypocritical too, even as they dismay at the corruption around them. Michael's words to Devin about outsourcing and offshoring were not a critique of specific economic procedures that could be politically opposed, but a depthless sound bite signifying nothing but vague topical relevance, because a certain notion of "anti-capitalism" has traction with *GTAV*'s target audience. In one sense, the message here is more developed than in "naïve" critiques of capitalism which believe, for example, that greater democratic participation is all that is required to counter its ills. Yet it shows no appreciation of what capitalism and anti-capitalism mean in today's historical context, or the specific ways in which the latter might challenge the former. Similarly, Michael does not believe in his words to Devin, only in the superficiality of the modern world, and his own actions reinforce these beliefs.

No More Heroes: The City as Wasteland

No More Heroes (*NMH*) is another game set in a fictional US city, but one which offers a vision of US culture developed in Japan, and a significantly different approach to the open worlds of *SRIV* or *GTAV*. The usual split between free roaming and prescribed missions now takes shape in a far more surreal and self-reflexive universe, in which numerous "metanarrative" elements reference the game itself. Its overall tone is one of punkish rejection, depicted in its grimy visual style, barren city and cast of freakish characters. And the core mode of interaction is a deadly close combat that occurs at a remove from reality, where normal social rules are irrelevant and even death is greeted with disinterest. As with *GTAV*, *NMH* features a main character who struggles to find meaning in modern society (there are "no more heroes" perhaps because there are no more heroic causes), and as with *SRIV* he seeks that meaning in consumer culture. Yet, unlike *GTAV*, this protagonist still seems to *want* some greater sense of purpose, and, unlike *SRIV*, does not seem to really find it in his obsession with entertainment.

The main theme of *NMH* instead resides in how it reproduces and reflects on the real-world dynamics of playing the game within its own fiction. In particular, its main character's escape into a surreal, violent criminal underworld, which endows him with a clear life goal, mirrors the way we, as players, play the game to escape our commodified reality. That is, its power fantasy is one of evading dominant expectations and forging a path outside social norms, but it is complicated by the lack of a place to go that exists outside the capitalist totality. In effect, while all the games examined in this book can be seen as escapist power fantasies, *NMH* offers escapism itself as a power fantasy, in that it provides us and its main character with an alternate life that offers real meaning and satisfaction, even if we must eventually admit to ourselves that it is fake. In the end, there is thus no solution to modern alienation on offer here, only a temporary distance from it that brings some release before dumping us back in reality. In this way, *NMH* is implicitly critical of American and Japanese obsessions with consumer entertainment, and even considers its own position in that culture, by mocking its audience and provoking them to reflect on the false escape that playing it entails. But it doesn't imagine a political alternative to the desperate society, so this false escape is left as the only option for the dispossessed, or an understandable response to existing social conditions which is perhaps all we can achieve.

As an ideological response, this "escapist defeatism" contains elements of cynicism, in that it also involves an outward rejection of normal social demands and a pessimistic outlook. The difference between it and cynical self-interest, however, is that the defeatist doesn't still want to thrive within the existing order. Whereas cynical self-interest distances behaviour from moral values only to really enjoy following dominant demands after all, the defeatist is less excited by regular notions of success, but cannot imagine a way out. I believe this position embodies various features of what Mark Fisher calls "capitalist realism," which is less about competitive spirit or "making it" and more a kind of depressed state of low expectation within a totalizing capitalist reality. From this perspective, because there is no available social alternative, all that remains is to mentally block out reality, with the most alluring option to seek refuge within the products of capitalist consumer entertainment. Fisher in fact describes a condition of "depressive hedonia," where lost souls retreat into entertainment not because they expect the sense of fulfilment that the hedonist does, but because they see no other way to repel the drudgery of everyday life. As he says, this modern depression "is constituted not by an inability to get pleasure so much as it is by an inability to do anything else *except* pursue pleasure. There is a sense that 'something is missing' — but no appreciation that this mysterious, missing enjoyment can only be accessed *beyond* the pleasure principle."[22] And of course, the obsessive retreat into consumer pleasures only connects the defeatist even more deeply to the depressing reality, as it becomes part of the work-leisure cycle in which body and mind are allowed to relax, only to be rejuvenated for more draining labour. Even in strictly economic terms, if the escape is all we live for it still must be funded through labour; the only way to get more escape time is to return to the prison and earn it.

In *NMH*, this position is formulated through its main character, Travis Touchdown. As his absurdly Americanized name implies, this young man is an overt product of a stupefying modern consumer culture, yet precisely as such he seems utterly unequipped to deal with everyday adult life. Apparently lacking any significant education, work ethic, moral compass or interpersonal skills, Travis seems to reject most conventional aspirations (career, relationships, property). But also lacking the perception and streetwise sensibilities embodied in the *GTAV* characters, he is still "naïve" enough to seek a purpose. What this purpose is he is perhaps not self-aware enough to define, and instead appears to simply internalize values he has learned from consumer entertainment—perhaps the only clear path remaining that offers some sense of joy, no matter how empty. His life thus revolves around immature pursuits: videogames, collectable cards and anime merchandise, Mexican wrestling, porn, motorbikes, and "punk" style. These "geeky" cultural obsessions render him a social misfit, in that they eschew a healthy life balance and social interaction, but they are also products of mainstream society, intertwined with manufactured consumer ideals. This ambiguous social inclusion-exclusion of the escapist is hinted at from the beginning, in the slogan displayed under the logo of the game's development team, Grasshopper Manufacture: "Punk's not dead." The implied rebellion of this slogan seems simultaneously genuine and all too aware that it has already been re-incorporated into the commodified system of consumer styles. Similarly, with Travis, his impotent expression of individuality through mass-produced toys and ready-made fashions suggests that punk *is* dead, yet his extreme focus on these distractions really does in effect reject other social conventions and mock the absurdity of the status quo.

This ambiguous relationship between Travis and the social reality is further present throughout *NMH* in its audio-visual style and in the representation of its city, Santa Destroy. The game revels in its deliberately "b-tier" production values, with its washed-out colour, scratched film effect, crude dialogue and messy transitions between scenes. In this respect as much as any it is an anti-*Grand Theft Auto*, exhibiting its lowly position with pride against the supremely polished mega-franchise. Santa Destroy, meanwhile, is as the name implies: a bleak, west-coast American sprawl, or desolate, colourless wasteland in direct contradiction to the lively, noisy streets of Los Santos. It is an almost abstract representation, built from nondescript buildings and roads and sparsely populated by faceless sleepwalkers. This city is still an open world to be freely explored, but navigating its space, whether by motorbike or on foot, is an empty and largely pointless experience. Only a handful of buildings can be entered, from Travis's motel room home to the local video shop, clothing store, weapon shop, gym and job centre. There are some collectable items in the back alleys and dumpsters, and a few city landmarks break up the otherwise featureless street layouts, but no structures of play, risk and reward, or meaningful discovery. It appears rather that the city simply doesn't register Travis's presence at all. As a man with no social ties—no job, no property, no family,[23] no girlfriend, few friends—he is simply unwanted. But then, it is not as though Travis seems to be missing out on much anyway. The barren roads of Santa Destroy bear witness to the robotic drudgery and seedy corruption that is modern urban life, which can only fuel his desire to escape. Roaming freely in *NMH* thus resists the usual neoliberal connotations of the videogame city as a place to accumulate funds or create enjoyment. It reinforces Travis's sense of boredom and alienation, and the escapism of consumer entertainment is actually juxtaposed against this reality, in the game's prescribed missions.

The problem for Travis within this neoliberal wasteland is that, once the norms of life are rejected, he has no specific expectations, objectives or standards to meet. From what we are led to understand of Travis's life prior to the events of the game, he lacks any clear direction or directing authority to follow. His position then reflects the idea developed by Žižek through the terminology of psychoanalyst Jacques Lacan that, in placing increasing emphasis on personal responsibility for success and enjoyment, neoliberalized societies appear to have no "big Other," or no generalized symbolic guarantee of meaning that explicitly prescribes standards of behaviour. With no singular authoritative voice to aid our decision-making, the attraction of consumerist distractions is perhaps unsurprising, but as the seductive promises of consumer entertainment remain unfulfilled, the pressure remains on us to take responsibility for this dissatisfaction as well. Neoliberalism's constant demand to do more, without telling us *what* to do or where we might find it, means we are always guilty of failure, and can't really identify once and for all what we wish to become. In *NMH*, Travis thus only seems to have a vague notion of his ideal self, informed by an immature obsession with consumer entertainment, that he must somehow try to realize. So, while he rejects many dominant social prescriptions, and looks for meaning elsewhere, the neoliberal logic continues in the background to form his desires (fantasy idealizations of media archetypes: the videogame hero, the punk, the porn star) and his sense of guilt (for not assuming responsibility).

The plot of NMH then revolves around what happens when Travis finds a sense of meaning in his escapism, and what happens when he loses it again. The events are set in motion by his chance encounter one drunken night with the game's main NPC, Sylvia. In a brief opening sequence, Travis reveals how Sylvia introduced him to an organization of contract killers called the United Assassins Association (UAA). For some reason, she persuaded him to kill the UAA's "eleventh ranked" assassin, which has made Travis himself the new eleventh ranked assassin. But now, Sylvia explains, Travis is a target for other would-be assassins, so he should stay ahead of the game by going up the ranks further, which means killing the ten other assassins above him. Despite feeling tricked, Travis accepts and quickly embraces the challenge, and so progresses through the game forms around a series of "ranking matches" organized by Sylvia, each staged in a different location (baseball stadium, school, film studio), where Travis first fights a horde of faceless henchmen before battling the next ranked killer to the death. The structure of Travis's quest is of course that of a typical videogame, in which each location is a new "level" full of rank and file enemies, with a single, high-powered enemy, or "boss," waiting at the end.

So why does Travis throw himself into such a nonsensical challenge? In part because he is stupid and in part to impress the sexually alluring Sylvia, but mainly it seems because his life now has a tangible sense of purpose. That is, Travis's mission is not only structured like a videogame for the sake of the player; in the context of the narrative this move also creates a framework that Travis can recognize and identify with. It is precisely the kind of fantasy he escapes into by playing games that now becomes his reality. In psychoanalytic terms, Sylvia and the UAA assume the role of authority figures that structure Travis's desire and tell him how to enjoy, relieving him of that uncertainty. In other words, they take the form of the "big Other" that is absent in the neoliberal demand for personal responsibility. Indeed, it is not unusual in reality for individuals to seek a surrogate figure (such as a religion or a political cause) that provides ready-made answers and replaces the undeterminable sense of responsibility with a set of clearly defined duties. Similarly, before Sylvia, Travis is wandering in the dark, and by reinventing him as an assassin she reorganizes his ideological fantasy and provides him with a definite identity, ratified by an official external body. We can see this in the contrast between the aimlessness of roaming the desolate city and the organization of space in the ranking matches, which place Travis in visually distinct, architecturally varied locations, each with a single linear path to a goal. Here, he suddenly has a clear focus and aim, and the events that occur revolve solely around his agency. With these clear goals, Travis blindly follows Sylvia's rules with great enthusiasm, armed with a "beam katana" (a sort of light sabre), his knowledge of Mexican wrestling, and the irrepressible confidence of an indestructible videogame protagonist, regardless of the absurdity and murderous violence involved.

The goal of becoming the top-ranked assassin thus takes over Travis's life. In Lacanian psychoanalytic terms, it is his *"objet petit a,"* or the object of his desire that, once perceived, seems to him to have always been the goal of his existence. The meaning and importance that he bestows upon this aim comes entirely from his own cognition, no matter how heavily inspired by Sylvia, but appears to him as an absolute commandment. Travis becomes a kind of modern day Don Quixote: a moron whose brain has been addled by trashy pop culture and who now believes he has an important quest to fulfil. Sylvia simply fuels his fantasy (she goads him before each ranking match, daring him to enter "the garden of madness," and even says she may have sex with him should he reach number one) and watches him go. What is less clear is whether Travis is actually motivated by the violence itself. He certainly enjoys the fighting, but seems completely desensitized to its consequences, and (again like Don Quixote) is more obsessed with the codes of engagement he has gleaned from popular culture, especially videogames, that structure his understanding of what he is doing. In particular, it is the challenge of advancing through and completing the game that is important. As he progresses, he seems less interested in the sheer thrill of combat and more interested in a fair fight to test and prove his skills. He expresses respect for the honourable assassins and disgust for those who are decadent or cowardly. He is angered when one of his targets is killed by a third party, even though it still counts as a win, and even spares the life of another target, a young girl, ostensibly because she is not enough of a challenge. The consistent logic here is that of the difficult videogame, in which players seek an initially insurmountable challenge and find satisfaction in learning how to beat it.

The other important aspect of this set up, and the one that mocks us as players the most, is that throughout the game Sylvia demands large sums of money from Travis to set up each match. It is this need to earn money, as well as improve skills and weapons, that forces Travis to traverse the city and visit its few significant locations. This financial demand imposed on Travis from Sylvia, and therefore on the player in the game, actually stops both from simply getting on with the ranking matches. And because Travis has to fund his fantasy, including Sylvia's expenses, the assassins' fees and so on, his escape from reality is still tied to the regular economy. *NMH* highlights how consumerist escapist fantasies must be funded by the very normality we wish to escape, and the deeper the escape the more funding is required. The paradox is represented superbly in the kind of jobs Travis must do between matches. While there are extra contract killing jobs on offer, the game only grants access to these *after* the player completes more menial tasks taken from the local job centre, from picking coconuts and mowing lawns to collecting litter and cleaning graffiti. At these points, Travis is plunged back into an ideological normalcy where work is deemed valuable and fulfilling, as the job centre official we encounter frames each activity in spiritual terms. As he explains of litter picking: "Each piece of garbage is a lost soul. So what better way to spend your life? Saving lost souls! A true garbage man can bring peace to the dead!" Naturally, we ignore such ideas, but we must still relinquish our agency to diligently do the work to pay for the fantasy, and even find ourselves trying to perform as best we can, to maximize our gain.

Even more interesting, however, is that all of these elements are upended by a final twist near the end of the game. After many battles, and having climbed his way up to second place in the assassin rankings, Travis discovers that the UAA is nothing but an elaborate hoax created by Sylvia, who operates such schemes to maintain her high-class hedonistic lifestyle. Prior to the final match, Travis phones Sylvia, only for her mother to answer (although the voice is suspiciously similar to Sylvia's) and explain the truth about her daughter, who has done this sort of thing before. The reason the structure of the matches so closely follows Travis's fantasies is that it was designed for him (and possibly others like him), after Sylvia ascertained he was a perfect victim for the swindle on their first meeting. As such, not only has all that labour served to line the pockets of a wealthy socialite (the game's exploitative capitalist), but the actual quest itself is robbed of its meaning. And yet, when Travis discovers he has been duped, with very little persuasion he decides to continue and enter the final battle regardless. After explaining the scam Sylvia's mother adds: "So just one more to go... Alrighty. Why not play along since you've come this far?" Travis responds with incredulity: "Are you serious? What's the point? This is all some make-believe charade." Sylvia's mother again appeals to the meaning he understands: "But a good man finishes what he started. Fight to the end!" Travis has not actually been an assassin, and his achievements were never "real," but there is still a challenge to beat that cannot be abandoned.

What is significant here in psychoanalytic terms is that Travis sticks to his object of desire, even without reason. To begin with, reaching number one is a goal that promises some sort of "official" recognition by an external "Other" or symbolic authority. But, once the reality created by Sylvia is revealed as false, Travis takes enjoyment from the process itself. The absence of meaning doesn't change Travis's desire, and he continues to pursue it with the same intensity. Again, this point reflects back on the player, in a way that also mirrors the relationship between character and reader in *Don Quixote*. In the latter, the metanarrative "tricks" the reader into taking its fiction seriously, or trying to make sense of things that never add up (who exactly wrote this supposedly true history, and how did he witness it all?), while presenting us with a pitiful main character who embodies the folly of doing exactly the same. Similarly, players of *NMH* (who might typically share some of Travis's "geeky" interests) endeavour to meet its objectives, struggle to follow its increasingly nonsensical narrative, and enjoy their violent escape from reality, all while laughing at the hapless Travis for doggedly pursuing his meaningless achievement.

To understand Travis's willingness to continue more closely, we can further "psychoanalyze" his ideological condition. In particular, despite the sense of fulfilment Travis gains from victories on his quest, he seems haunted by a sense of incompleteness or longing that he cannot explain. In the tenth place ranking match, Travis battles an ageing assassin in his huge mansion, surrounded by symbols of material wealth. As Travis fights he muses through an internal monologue that he is looking at his potential future self. At first he concludes, "It's the perfect life. It's the life for winners. That'll be my life!" But perhaps it is not *his* perfect life after all. He continues:

I realize there's really nothing here for me. But what else can I do but keep going? Maybe I should have been a little more careful before I jumped in. Gotta find the exit. Gotta find that exit to Paradise. But, I can't see it. Can't see anything. There's this sense of doom running down my spine, like it's…Like it's trying to suck the life out of me. I need to get rid of it before I bail. Something deeper…deeper than my instincts is taunting me. Can't find the exit. Can't find the exit. Can't find the exit. Can't find the exit. Can't find the exit.

That "something deeper" may be seen in psychoanalytic terms as "death drive," or a kind of gap in our subjective identities that means we are never quite fully reconciled with ourselves. It is an inevitable sense of uncertainty that emerges because there is no final truth about what things mean, only different understandings that emerge in human consciousness through language. No matter how knowledgeable we are, each of us only has our own perspective and cannot know the innermost feelings and thoughts of others. Moreover, our own deepest desires are not even compatible (for example, the desires for risk and security), so that satisfying one may leave us unsatisfied in another way. In short, nothing is ever really, conclusively fulfilling, and our ideological fantasies which make us feel that there is some absolute meaning merely distract us from that realization. For Travis, it seems that "if only" he could reach number one he would achieve an inexhaustible victory, but even early on he also feels that this is not quite enough, that there is an undefinable something else.

As the game ends, Travis enters a new fight, and clashes swords with his new opponent, irrespective of rules or rankings, with apparently no delusions about any greater meaning. His final line: "Then let's find that exit they call Paradise." The concept of "Paradise" is one that Travis alludes to repeatedly in *NMH*. In that early fight in the mansion he refers to it as "the place where dreams are fulfilled," but then also exclaims "Here's your ticket to Paradise" as he kills his opponent. In this way we can see Paradise for Travis as the place where he finds meaning, but also ultimately the only place where that longing feeling really stops: death. In the game's last moment, the "exit" of Paradise thus seems to signify both the temporary escapism realized in the fight itself, and that final exit of death. In Lacanian psychoanalysis, drive is effectively split between the unending sense of longing and partial fulfilment gained by trying and failing to reach the object of desire, which stands in for and obscures the void of meaning. At some level, Travis seems to understand that there is no final goal, but that by continuing to act as if there is he can still reproduce the loop of partial satisfaction that helps repress the longing. In effect, for Travis, the "goal" of trying to be number one sets in motion the "aim," which becomes that of getting enjoyment from the fighting itself. Similarly, for players, the game structure promises satisfaction should we beat it, but then of course simply ejects us back into reality, to search for the next distraction. We know that this will happen, but act as if the goal was real for the duration of the game, so we can enjoy the aim of playing it.

The other aspect of the death drive does not disappear, however, and still pushes against the fantasy structure through which Travis organizes his enjoyment. In Žižek's words, death drive also designates "the desperate endeavour to escape the clutches of the 'undead' eternal life, the horrible fate of being caught in the endless repetitive cycle of *jouissance*."[24] Thus, even if Travis has accepted that he fights purely for the temporary escapism it brings, he still won't fully shake the "sense of doom" that taunts him. Yet the important point here from the perspective of ideology analysis is not that he should be able to find real fulfilment, as this indiscernible longing is inherent to human subjectivity, but that he doesn't interpret the lack of meaning revealed by Sylvia's deceit as a kind of liberation, or an opportunity to redefine his identity on his own terms. Instead, his imagination remains caught within the confines of consumer entertainment, accepting its fleeting thrills to be as good as it gets. Of course, it is consistent with Travis as a character that he should learn little of consequence in his adventure, and in taking this route *NMH* is very prescient about the function of ideology, or the way people often cling to their position in the end just because, regardless of reason. But at the same time, by not interrogating the cultural background that structures Travis's fantasy, its dense meta-critique leaves no room for any fantasy that goes beyond neoliberal concepts of personal responsibility and identity creation through consumerist enjoyment. The neoliberal background is then still all there is; the idea that there is no alternative fantasy remains as an unexamined assumption, and any self-evaluation of desire foreclosed. This assumption affirms the idea that we are isolated individuals unable to affect change through collective political aims, and temporary escape remains the only form of rebellion. If Travis's new attitude helps him reject the neoliberal guilt trip that holds him responsible for not finding complete fulfilment, it is replaced by a punishing demand to continually find bigger and more deadly challenges, until death.

Travis's pursuit of excitement and danger is not the hedonism of *SRIV*, but a fantasy that resigns itself to the moderate satisfaction of enjoyable failure. This is perhaps a condition prevalent in all mass consumerism, in that it does not necessarily dupe individuals into thinking its products will really fulfil them, but offers an appealing option in a society that otherwise rarely registers their agency. It is an alternative acceptance of consumerism defined by individuals' desire for distraction, because it is too hard to actually change the existing reality. The contrast between *SRIV*'s hedonism and *NMH*'s escapist defeatism is located here, in the way the consumer simultaneously enjoys or is gratified by the experience and knows it is ineffectual and largely meaningless, but welcomes the deception nonetheless. In *NMH*, Travis invites that partial and empty satisfaction, but seems ready to die for it as much as he wishes it to continue, because he cannot think beyond neoliberal ideas to alternative concepts of fulfilment.

6

Persona 5: The City as Prison

Persona 5 (*P5*) offers a different gaming experience to the other games examined in this book. First, it isn't an open-world action game but a Japanese "RPG" or role-playing game. As such, it places heavy emphasis on storyline, dialogue and character development, and combines this with "turn-based" tactical combat in which the player controls a whole party of characters at once, selecting their actions from menus, and then watching the results unfold. Second, within *P5*'s city, a stylized representation of Tokyo, players are more restricted in their movements, with each district recreated as a small, enclosed area containing points of prescribed interaction (conversation, shopping, and various work or leisure activities) accessible only at given times. It is not then how we traverse the city that is important, as movement between areas is instant, but how we choose to spend the limited slots of time provided. Third, the sense of routine created in its carefully structured time and space is very much part of *P5*'s ideological outlook, as what is also different from the other games here is that its characters explicitly *want* to be part of mainstream society and the neoliberal work-leisure cycle. The main protagonist and his friends do not resent the pressure to maximize their time *as such*, or juggle school work, social life, consumerist pursuits and social responsibilities, only that their attempts at individual expression and self-realization are unfairly blocked. In the representations of American life we have so far seen, it is the absence of social structure that creates existential issues. Conversely, the problem for this group of teenagers in Japanese society is that hierarchies are still too rigid and stifling. They find themselves lost not due to the bewildering nature of neoliberalism's demands, which still make sense to them, but because those demands are corrupted by greed and cynicism.

The plot of *P5* then sees this group become united by a sense of injustice, and pulls them into a bizarre parallel dimension through which they can affect change to make the system work as intended. With this fantasy, *P5* thus also stands out from the other games because its message is more overtly political. More specifically, it signifies a "rebellion" against elite abuse of a social hierarchy based around age and status: the lack of voice given to the young, the demand for unquestioning obedience, and the failure of adult authorities to confront corruption. But with its underlying acceptance of neoliberal life goals, this rebellion only confronts issues of personal responsibility and moral failing, rather than questioning political and economic systems. In the end, in *P5*, it is not the institutions that are at fault, but the cynical individuals that abuse them and the public apathy that lets the cynics get away with it. The power fantasy that emerges is a reformist ideal, in which change means reinvigorating the public's sense of social responsibility to remove the corrupt elites obstructing the smooth flow of systems. However, in presenting social problems in terms of personal psychological issues, *P5* must still explain why *so many* people in its world are corrupt or apathetic. Without any systemic analysis to support its critique, the game frames social decline as the result of a great conspiracy among the elite, and even otherworldly forces. We then encounter various individuals in *P5*, including educators, legal professionals, politicians, corporate CEOs and famous artists, who personify corruption, enabling a fantasy in which the heroes (via their own supernatural powers) get to name and confront the source of social ills, and make the culprits confess their crimes.

At the core of the reformist dream presented in *P5* is a desire for everyone to be able to "enjoy responsibly," as long as one person's enjoyment or ambition doesn't curtail anybody else's. As such, what is socially important is to support neoliberal demands with checks and balances to ensure that everyone has access to career and lifestyle choices. For this ideological position, political responsibility is a central part of daily life, beyond the individualistic prescriptions of neoliberalism; it is not unaware of social problems, and nor does it simply ignore them or admit defeat. And as for *how* to improve the existing system and make it run smoothly, its underlying faith is in democracy and the power of the people, *if only* they can be inspired to fully engage with social matters. It also has faith in persuasion, or that through higher standards in politics, education and the media, a public may emerge that can fulfil its social duty. Yet what is missing here is any appreciation of the extent to which neoliberalized political, financial, legal and cultural institutions themselves cause social disengagement, or how the logic of profit actively works against deeper democratic participation. In other words, it does not ask whether democracy may itself be problematic in its existing form, or whether people might be politically disengaged because of privatized media's tendency to trivialize politics, the influence of corporate money on political parties, or the excessive demands on other aspects of their lives. Indeed, meaningful political change is unlikely, as Jodi Dean points out, when "the appeal to democracy presupposes democracy is the solution to the problems of democracy, because it incorporates in advance any hope things might be otherwise as already the fundamental democratic promise and provision."[25] Since the promise of freedom is already present in the current form of democracy, it seems there is no reason to look for it elsewhere, or consider how that freedom may be stunted by the institutions it seeks to revitalize.

In accordance with these ideas, the major themes in *P5*'s narrative and interactive structures are imprisonment and freedom. The story begins as the main character (named by the player) arrives in Tokyo from his small home town to enrol in an elite prep school. In flashbacks we learn that, due to the actions of a particularly corrupt and powerful individual, he has been wrongly convicted of assault and expelled from his local high school, and is now on probation with a criminal record. With this undeserved reputation for violence he is met with distrust in his new temporary home, and told unequivocally he must avoid further trouble or go to prison for real. Consequently, at the start of the game, the character's (and player's) movements are closely watched and heavily restricted, as well as regulated by time, with each portion of the day assigned specific activities. The city environment thus symbolizes our prison, with more locations and choices gradually made available to us as privileges as the character appears to be fitting in. No matter how much freedom we gain, however, the in-game calendar continues to enforce its schedule of school attendance, plot-related events and "free time" for leisure activities, socializing or studying.

Naturally, *P5* is not merely about being a responsible student, and the narrative soon introduces a supernatural element with a parallel dimension called the "Metaverse," in which the main character is tasked with achieving a different kind of "rehabilitation." The Metaverse is a dimension that manifests people's unconscious cognition, or the deeply repressed fantasies that motivate their behaviour beneath conscious perception. Clearly there are parallels with psychoanalysis here, and in fact the *Persona* series as a whole is especially influenced by Carl Jung's theories of the psyche, which include the concept of the "persona" itself. In this case, themes of identity and self-imprisonment are explored through the player's main objective of entering the Metaverse to alter the desires of certain particularly corrupt individuals, in order to stop their abuses of power in reality. As a result, the normal routines of schoolwork and social life intertwine with these visits to the Metaverse, so that all responsibilities must be successfully managed if the character (and the new friends he makes) are to enjoy their freedom and realize their potentials.

The villainous individuals whose desires must be changed have their own personalized locations in the Metaverse called "Palaces," which manifest their deepest fantasies. The first of these is Kamoshida, a PE teacher and ex-Olympic volleyball medallist, who bullies the academy's volleyball players and eventually even sexually assaults a member of the girls' team. The students are powerless to resist—his behaviour is almost an open secret in the school, tolerated by the headmaster and even parents because of the prestige associated with the team. In the Metaverse, Kamoshida's unconscious recreates the school as a castle, where he is the king and the team his slaves. His conscious self is unaware of the castle's existence, but it, and his "shadow"[26] form that dwells inside, represent his underlying desires and motivations. The main character and two other students find themselves in this castle, where they also meet Morgana, a mysterious talking cat who conveniently explains the situation. Most importantly, it transpires, within every Palace is a "treasure," or an object with which its ruler is obsessed (another instance of Lacan's "*objet petit a*" that organizes desire). In Kamoshida's case this is his crown, which symbolizes his Olympic medal in reality, and through it his sense of superiority within the school. Yet this treasure is also the Palace owner's weakness, as it structures their cognition, so if the characters can infiltrate the Palace and steal it, they will force the Palace owner to have a "change of heart" in reality.

This premise provides us with a series of typical videogame quests to complete, as to reach a treasure the main character and his friends must overcome various obstacles and battle other "shadows" that take the form of monsters when approached. And to do that each must connect with his/her spirit of rebellion in the form of a "persona," a mythological embodiment of one's innermost unconscious fantasies. The Personas in *P5* in fact effectively reverse the Jungian concept, as for Jung our persona is the "mask" that we wear to interact with the outside world and conform to social expectations. In *P5*, conversely, the initial problem for the characters is really that their masks are too strong: they struggle to express their personal feelings of injustice because they are so conditioned to respect the social hierarchy. The emergence of each character's persona in the game then actually signifies what Jung would call the "disintegration" of the persona. They all reach a point at which the frustrations of their own conformist subservience become too great to bear, and literally go through a violent act of tearing off a mask that appears stuck to their face. With this act they unleash their individual personality, including aspects of their repressed unconscious fantasies, and remain in an alternate guise as long as they are within the Metaverse (while in the real world this change helps them to psychologically balance their social assimilation and individual identity). They can now fight the cognitive apparitions in the Palaces and steal the treasures, causing the real-world Kamoshida and other villains to feel guilt, confess their crimes publicly and demand punishment.

After successfully changing Kamoshida's heart, the group's reputations and ambitions grow, and as they do *P5*'s plot assumes a more political dimension. Calling themselves the "Phantom Thieves," the main character and an expanding circle of friends seek out higher profile targets to affect social change, such as an organized crime boss and a corporate CEO, before finally going after a corrupt politician named Shido, who is set to become Prime Minister of Japan. The idea in *P5* of accessing one's individuality and rebellious side becomes a genuine demand for progressive social reform. The supernatural forces that have given the main character access to the Metaverse designate him as a "trickster,"[27] or the joker in the pack that can push back the apparently inexorable tide of corruption. This trickster could also be seen as the embodiment of society's excluded or oppressed, or those who snap back because they cannot reconcile the dominant rhetoric and its professed values with their own oppressed situation. Accordingly, *P5*'s power fantasy fights for the exploited and downtrodden, here represented as the youth. It also emphasizes collective agency, in the way the strength of the Phantom Thieves increases as new members join, and the main character forges deeper bonds with them and other "confidants" he meets. And finally, it shows us that the elites themselves are not the only problem, as Shido is eventually made to confess his sins, yet nobody seems to care. At this point, the Phantom Thieves realize that the true magnitude of the task of social reform is to change the public unconscious itself. They must enter a part of the Metaverse called "Mementos," which represents a kind of mass cognition, to inspire the public into action.

In this way, *P5*'s message revolves around three different psychological types, two of which are prisoners to their self-interest, and one of which is a self-reflexive free subject, on whom it falls to liberate the others. Of course, the free subject is exemplified by the Phantom Thieves themselves, and the main character's confidants. These (mostly young) people are morally motivated, confront their personal flaws, and learn to take responsibility for a just society. As for the other two types, one is represented by the general public, who are shown to be uncommitted, fickle, apathetic and ignorant individuals that may want a just society, but take no responsibility for it. In what Žižek calls the "culture of complaint" in modern societies, they constantly ask some authority figure to make life better, and even "enjoy" playing the perpetual victim, effectively recognizing themselves as subordinates, rather than as agents who could actually affect change. Likewise, in *P5*, public opinion first imagines the Phantom Thieves as saviours, but later disowns them when they appear to have become too radical, and when Shido promises to restore order through conventional political means. The final psychological type is embodied in characters such as Kamoshida, Shido and most of the other Palace owners.

71

These are a minority of self-interested cynics (as in *GTAV*) in positions of power, who decide to aggressively impose their wills on society, realizing that most people will simply not resist. Effectively, in this situation, the Phantom Thieves are dangerous not because they *threaten* official moral standards, but because they take them seriously when everyone else doesn't. The Phantom Thieves refuse or fail to recognize the unwritten rules of society, which tell people when to obey the official rules and when to ignore them, causing the whole symbolic infrastructure to wobble.

While there is certainly something challenging in *P5*'s concept of self-determination and the agency of the oppressed leading to social change, in many ways it doesn't fully get to grips with the issues it introduces. To begin with, the inspirational message of political agency and responsibility it pushes relies too heavily on the game's supernatural plot devices. For sure, as with the other games here, *P5* is not trying to be a political manifesto, merely an artistic representation of social issues, and it can hardly be expected to answer questions about how to facilitate social change that even seasoned political theorists struggle with. As mentioned in the introduction, Jameson's notion of "cognitive mapping" highlights how difficult it is, with all the complexities of the (post)modern age, to understand the social structures and forces that affect our lives. With no such "map" available, culture is limited to allegorical representations, and in *P5* we see one of the main forms Jameson identifies: the conspiracy theory. The value of imagining social degradation as the fault of a shady cabal of authority figures and supernatural forces is that it grants a sense of a complete picture, or "closure" that "is the sign that somehow all the bases have been touched, and that the galactic dimensions and co-ordinates of the now global social totality have at least been sketched in."[28] And even though it fails to understand the social totality, it at least reveals a continuing attempt to do so, or to rethink how things work. But this approach also seems to reinforce a notion that meaningful political change requires external intervention, from forces beyond human control, to enable the people to take action, which grates against its explicit message.

The Metaverse thus functions for much of the game as a convenient tool to resolve a block in political imagination. Most obviously, the whole reason that the Phantom Thieves must change their targets' desires through the Palaces is because they are powerless in reality. And then, towards the end of the game, when Shido's public confession is met with mass disinterest rather than anger, and it seems that this public apathy will thwart the rebellion, the narrative again turns to the supernatural, and a *deus ex machina* in the shape of a "god" who reveals itself to have orchestrated the whole scenario. This god, "Yaldabaoth," has been brought into being by the public's indolence, and resides as the treasure at the heart of Mementos, in the form of the Holy Grail. The heart of Mementos itself manifests central Tokyo literally as a prison, in which the people's shadows are happy prisoners, satisfied with their daily drudgery as long as they don't need to think for themselves. It also turns out that Yaldabaoth is the force that tasked the main character with "rehabilitation" from the start, that is, the rehabilitation of humanity from its corruption and apathy. It now judges that the trickster has failed, confirming its suspicion that humans are beyond redemption, and begins to destroy the city by fusing it with the Metaverse. Yet because of this we have something concrete to fight once again, and so the Phantom Thieves eventually inspire the people to support them, making it possible to beat Yaldabaoth. In this case, the people's change of heart does not entail forcibly altering their unconscious, as they will the Phantom Thieves to win *against* the being that their own desire created. But we should note here that the existential threat caused by Yaldabaoth's judgement doesn't exactly leave the people with any other alternative; they abandon apathy in the end only because it is no longer effective in maintaining the status quo. The conditions of change are therefore realized purely because of the supernatural upheaval, with no relatable parallel in reality.

Another deeper ideological issue to consider, which also explains why *P5* relies on the Metaverse so much in its vision of social change, is its strictly psychological treatment of politics. In other words, its notions of reform revolve around *individuals*, albeit in great numbers, committing to self-reflection and taking responsibility for their desires, rather than considering how those desires are shaped by social norms and institutions. This approach mirrors the neoliberal focus on personal weakness as a cause of social ills, and the need to alter our thinking and character traits to meet social demands. In *P5*, although the problems of apathy and corruption are clearly so prevalent that they affect the vast majority of people, the solution is still one of personal improvement. Perhaps the most obvious question it leaves unanswered is: if Yaldabaoth is the manifestation of mass resignation and irresponsibility, why did these traits become so overwhelming *now* that they brought the god into being? The Phantom Thieves stand for agency and self-determination; as Morgana says, "Humans have the power to change the world. They just forgot about that a bit..." But what made them forget? What is it about modern society specifically that caused such widespread forgetting? What is to stop it happening again? What if the apathy is a result of a modern life where active engagement seems useless, because all those consumer, lifestyle and even voting decisions are only superficially effective? *P5* does not ask these questions. It reveals a rot throughout the institutions, from education and culture, to business, law and politics, but only in terms of the elite conspirators who must be cleansed from the system and a public failing to remember its civic duty.

In merely demanding a populace that is more politically vigilant and active, then, *P5* cannot imagine itself out of the boundaries of neoliberal expectations. It seems unable to visualize existing political and economic systems, and the life priorities they engender, as part of a liberal capitalist social background that could be examined and even questioned. Indeed, the way the player interacts with the game also reinforces acceptance of social norms and routines surrounding jobs, relationships and consumer pleasures that effectively makes them universal facts of life.[29] The rules and objectives of *P5* challenge players to efficiently organize the protagonist's development within a limited number of time slots. The structuring of time and the activities available each day follow the prescriptions of normality and authority, and assume an extreme rigidity. In some cases, we have no choice in what to do (attend school, observe a plot development) at other times we are allowed to select an activity that accords with the time of day or year, and other people's schedules. We are told when to get up, when we have a day off, and when to go to bed, and each choice we make is monitored and recorded. That is, everything we do in *P5* is reduced to a calculable value, as not only studying or performing chores, but even leisure pursuits, such as going to the cinema, eating out, or fishing are measured in terms of how they improve the character's personal attributes (knowledge, charm and so on) or social relationships. With these time pressures and systems of measurement, *P5* really embodies how freedom to choose in modern society is regulated by a demand to realize our potentials in every way, and how there is never enough time to do so. In representing the routines of daily life in game form it recreates the stress of being faced with constant decisions, all of which appear equally urgent.

Furthermore, the apparent escape from reality that is the Metaverse, in which the characters unleash their unconscious Personas, increasingly becomes more like a kind of labour that must be done to earn free time in reality. In effect, it is a reversal of *NMH*'s insistence on the player labouring in the real world before being allowed to escape into the fantasy. The game's structure revolves around specific "deadlines" by which treasures must be stolen, and each of the seven Palaces we enter is larger and more labyrinthine than the last. And despite the opportunity to explore, fight and overcome obstacles in the Palaces, and their impressively imaginative design, in practice they are repetitive, drawn out and not taxing enough to hold attention. In fact, time can literally grind to a halt in the Metaverse, as each visit takes up a single afternoon in reality, no matter how long the player spends there. This also means that, although players do not have to finish Palaces in one go, it makes sense to try and get them out of the way in one long slog, because each new visit eats up potential socializing time in the outside world. The result of all this is that enjoyment in *P5* is found less in the act of assuming an alter ego and entering a supernatural dimension to battle evil and change the world, and more in the daily "freedoms" of deciding when to socialize, eat, read and so on that become rewards for meeting deadlines. Certainly, this is not simply a case of celebrating consumer freedoms, as the prison at the heart of Mementos shows us the trap of focusing only on our daily activities. Rather, while the social responsibility signified by the Metaverse is a chore, it is a *necessary* chore, that should supplement our daily routine, no matter how risky and daunting but also tiresome or inconvenient it may be, in order to maximize our everyday lifestyle choices.

It should not be forgotten that *P5* retains a politically charged message and a powerful response to cynicism. It tells us that we do not have to accept social relations as they are or interpret them in a prescribed way, exemplified in the quote I mentioned at the beginning of this book: "If you want to change the world, all you have to do is just look at it differently." However, in both narrative and structure it falls short of its own aims. In the game's epilogue, the situation is optimistic; a character named Sae, the public prosecutor now pursuing Shido's case, explains to the teenage characters that, due to "civil protests, some of the more indecisive prosecutors came to our side," and "this is the first step to true change." She adds: "All that remains is for us adults to lead society in the right direction...Then again, I have to wonder if you believe what I say." But since the Metaverse no longer exists, whether they believe it or not, the gang has no real choice except to put their trust back in "the adults" (the elite authorities and the public). Fortunately, their defeat of Yaldabaoth has triggered mass psychological reform, revitalizing existing social systems and "rehabilitating" democracy through a renewed sense of political responsibility, so the reformist dream seems complete. But then, to what extent does *P5* really look at the world differently? Has it not accepted the existing form of democracy without considering whether it is still fit for purpose? Why not also question our dominant conceptions of freedom, and whether they contributed to the corruption and apathy in the first place? Without looking at these issues, can the current situation last?

Indeed, if we look closer, is there not something quite dogmatic about *P5*'s vision? Does it not actually imply a very specific expectation of social organization, which we are not supposed to deviate from or "look at differently?" As the game progresses, it is hard to shake the feeling that the themes of agency and social responsibility are merely a cover story for a group committed to imposing their own ideals at all costs. For example, the Phantom Thieves decide on their targets throughout much of the game by discussing each candidate as a group, with the proviso that they must be in unanimous agreement before entering that target's Palace. Yet these decisions are actually inevitable—baked into the prewritten narrative, with the player having no significant input in the conversation—so this democratic process is really only there for appearances sake. It is a way of *seeming* to contemplate all options, through rational deliberation that even notes ethical pitfalls, in order to officially endorse what was already decided.

It assumes that a free and open discussion leads to the outcome we knew was right all along, and that any measures, including interfering with someone's unconscious, are justified by the democratic seal of approval.

Moreover, while *P5* manages to prod at its central moral question through these discussions, it never fully grapples with the ramifications. That is: what does it really mean for the Phantom Thieves to steal someone's object of desire, which organizes their cognition and their identity as a conscious subject? As Morgana says early on, "desires are what we all need in order to survive. The will to sleep, eat, fall in love—those sorts of things. If all of those yearnings were to vanish, they'd be no different from someone who has shut down entirely." When the characters steal Kamoshida's treasure, the method is untested and they are uncertain exactly what will happen, but feel that the ends (stopping his abuses) justify the means. Fortunately, the result is as they had hoped, as the real Kamoshida confesses his crimes (it turns out that subjects only "shut down entirely" in reality if their shadow forms are killed in the Metaverse). But does that really make it acceptable? Surely, we have still erased the complexities of Kamoshida's mind and destroyed his personality, including his potential, no matter how remote, to change of his own accord. Or, is the point that we are all constructs of our unconscious, and that free will is an illusion? But if so, do we have any more right to free him from one unconscious fantasy only to place him under the control of another? Later in the game, the Phantom Thieves find the shadows of Kamoshida, Shido and some of the other villains within the Mementos prison, glad to now be free of their ambitions and cruel desires. Did the Phantom Thieves not condemn them to this?

What is especially troubling here is how perversity and corruption are described in *P5* as signs of a "distorted heart" which "indulges desire" (defined in very traditional terms, as each Palace represents one of the seven deadly sins), because this implies the possibility of an "undistorted" psyche that does not indulge desire. In psychoanalysis, conversely, we are all motivated by desire and all desire is pathological; there is no pure "heart" which pre-exists or resists social and personal conditioning. In a sense, desire is the *necessary* distortion of the lack of any truth that enables us to construct a worldview at all, regardless of whether society tells us it is noble or contemptible. Consequently, although the Phantom Thieves really do save people from the individuals they target, their notion of erasing distortion reflects a kind of puritanical absolute morality that cannot fully examine its own desire in turn.

Near the end of the game, as Yaldabaoth threatens to destroy Tokyo and the Phantom Thieves face defeat, each character experiences self-doubt about their strength and resolve to fulfil the task given to them, and whether they went far enough, yet their moral certitude seems unwavering. It thus appears that they were motivated not so much by a repressed sense of rebellion as by a strong sense of duty. Perhaps, in hindsight, their Personas were not manifestations of unconscious drive that broke free from tradition to create room for the new after all, but of a punishing "superego" that demands obedience to a specific moral code, and constantly chastises the subject for failing to be sufficiently loyal. It is only when the Metaverse and the Personas eventually disappear that this impossible demand retreats, at least temporarily. In the game's end sequence, the main character is due to return to his home town, but his friends decide to take him on a farewell road trip, which at last frees them from the restrictions of the city and the calendar. But what is this freedom but one final retreat into irresponsible youth, before they must all return home to become adults and resume the normal routine? *P5* frames imprisonment as apathy, resignation, acceptance, yet its characters and players must compliantly submit to its routines in order to advance.

7

Conclusion: Conformism and Critique

Throughout the preceding chapters I have aimed to define a range of psychological responses to neoliberalized social conditions, through their representation in videogames. The examples I have presented obviously depict exaggerated and abstracted versions of ideas and arguments we may encounter in everyday life, not least because they are all power fantasies in some sense. But they can still be especially useful in understanding how modern ideological positions function, precisely *because* they clearly reveal many of the unspoken beliefs and assumptions people rely on today, either when considering social and political issues, or simply deciding how to get on in life. In short, cultural products such as these games often symbolize big ideas, and sometimes work through them, whether by featuring characters who reflect on their purpose in life, or by framing stories and objectives as antagonistic oppositions of right and wrong. We can therefore gain valuable insights into the social psychology of the historical moment by examining its culture. So, even if these responses to neoliberalism don't exist in exactly these forms in reality, we can see them as archetypes of positions that people really do hold, and through them understand the kinds of justifications that attach people to the status quo.

Another related point here is that I don't see the four positions I have defined as an exhaustive list of responses to neoliberalism, as if they apply to everyone who lives roughly in accordance with modern social norms. We could easily expand the list further, for example by considering how more traditionalist or conservative beliefs function in modern societies, even becoming revitalized in new religious or nationalist movements. And such positions need not be seen merely as leftovers of a pre-neoliberal age, but themselves symptoms of neoliberalism, or responses that simultaneously reject its sense of identity fluidity and the absence of an overt authority figure, while revelling in its continuing socio-economic hierarchies, patriarchy and culture of blame.[30] My argument at this stage, however, is simply that there are a variety of psychological responses to neoliberal demands, and that the demands in fact engender such varied responses due to their relative openness and complexity. As such, it should also be clear that I don't see any particular ideological position as especially dominant or representative of mass consciousness today. For example, I don't believe that we are predominantly a society of cynics, who are all acutely aware of how the world (mal)functions but accept it nonetheless. In this case, while it is true that *GTAV* is by far the biggest selling of the games examined here, at least in the West, it's impossible to say how much that is down to its ideological resonance. Besides, the less cynical approaches of *SRIV* and *P5* (invested in the consumerist dream and the democratic ideal, respectively) are far from unfamiliar to us.

So how do these ideological positions manifest themselves in modern life? How do they relate to the characteristics identified in the games' power fantasies? To begin with "hedonism," in the context of neoliberalism I am thinking of a lifestyle that focuses substantially on consumerist entertainment or pleasure. This hedonist need not be an extreme thrill seeker or a wild party-goer. It would be equally "hedonistic," in the sense I am defining here, for someone to fixate on what they might want for dinner every night, be genuinely excited about seeing the latest superhero movie, or constantly want to go shopping. In this way, for this hedonist, work is predominantly a means to an end that must be done to pay for enjoyment. The hedonist wouldn't think twice about stopping work if they came into a large amount of money, but until then work is on balance a good thing, because it enables the purchase of pleasurable goods and services. At the same time, many big social issues, including politics, would appear boring to the hedonist. It is of course better when the economy is thriving, but it makes more sense to leave that stuff to the experts. In all this, such hedonism is not necessarily motivated by pure self-interest. Rather, it involves lines of rationalization based on neoliberal ideas, including consumerist concepts of identity creation but also an understanding of freedom in individual terms and a notion that there are no political alternatives. Moreover, it can justify itself in the sense that it doesn't do any harm, and that, if everyone were a hedonist, there wouldn't be any tribal politics or warmongering. Of course, what this argument represses is any connection between the availability of cheap and plentiful consumer goods and the poverty, slave labour, environmental decline and sense of meaninglessness it can engender.

With "cynical self-interest," meanwhile, we are looking at a position that is more informed about how things work, and certainly doesn't believe the official PR of big business and mainstream politics. Yet while it recognizes the hypocrisy when powerful figures claim to be acting in the best interests of all, it has no time for radical critique, whether left or right, that actually seeks significant changes to the status quo. Instead, the cynic wants things to stay as they are and to exploit them to his/her advantage. This self-interest is supported by pragmatic "realism." The market is flawed, so the argument goes, but better than the alternative; at least we aren't subjected to the oppressive and broken systems of, say, Soviet Russia or North Korea. We must remember that humans are a selfish and aggressive bunch, and grand social projects always fail, so we should make the most of what we have. There is of course a certain truth to this rhetoric, but it obscures that many people in the world still do have it bad, and that their situation is deeply connected to the wealth and freedoms elsewhere, so could improve under a different social order. Here, the cynic may claim that nothing can be done about this, or that someone somewhere always gets a raw deal, so we may as well just enjoy our luck. What is still missing, however, is any consideration that "human nature" has other aspects and adapts to different conditions, or that humans also share and act collectively, and are more likely to do so in more equal societies, where everyone has a stake and a reasonable quality of life. Central to cynicism is an idea that it rejects ideology for rationality, because ideologies are dogmatic and lead to authoritarianism. But with this alibi it fails to account for its own presumption of neoliberal ideas, particularly its onus on individual self-sufficiency and the impossibility of even *potentially* workable political or economic alternatives.

In "escapist defeatism" there is also recognition of social problems and also a notion that not much can be done about them, at least by the average citizen. It does perhaps entail more of a historical dimension than cynical self-interest, in focusing less on human nature and more on the way things are now, under a seemingly omnipotent global capitalist system. Moreover, for the defeatist, taking advantage of the situation isn't the most attractive option, because dominant notions of success simply don't seem that satisfying, or because an outward pursuit of self-interest remains ethically abhorrent. The only other alternative is thus to find points of distraction within the system, to block out the sense of alienation. The lure of consumer media is strong here, offering innumerable fantasy worlds and characters for defeatists to lose themselves in. Such media consumption goes beyond the throwaway pleasures of hedonism to a deeper identification with the chosen material, even if, deep down, the defeatist knows it is meaningless. This position most clearly relates to "geek" culture, focused on comic books, videogames, sci-fi/fantasy movies and so on, but could equally apply to certain sports fans or collectors of nostalgia. What is notable about these pursuits is both their "immaturity" (a kind of rejection of the adult world) and how heavily tied they are to the economy, forcing the individuals concerned back into the normalcy of work-leisure routines to financially maintain their obsession. Another possible aspect of this lifestyle is a kind of victim complex, in which the powers that be are held responsible for life's difficulties, but cannot be resisted, only mocked or angrily reproached. Either way, the defeatist does not take responsibility for his/her part in reproducing the status quo through excessive consumerist habits, or make any attempt to organize politically and create change.

Finally, the concept of "reformism" I have outlined revolves around an ideal of meritocracy, or a belief that everyone in society really should have the opportunity to "make it" and live the life they want, as long as it doesn't stop others doing the same. The reformist would not agree with the strict neoliberal notion that those who fail in current social circumstances are necessarily to blame for their plight, but would also not agree that the system itself is set up to cause these failures and is intrinsically unable to fulfil its promises. Instead, the answer is somewhere in between: the system works in principle but needs attention if it's ever going to run smoothly enough to produce a proper meritocracy. What is required, therefore, is collective vigilance and effort to get involved in improving the system, to stop anyone from having an overly corruptive impact. In short, no major overhaul is required, merely greater commitment to properly enforce the concepts of justice and equal opportunity that already exist. This position involves strong political commitment and a good working knowledge of existing systems. But it also implies strict adherence to a particular set of principles, specifically ones that do not question the actual political, social and economic institutions that are currently in place. In addition, the very idea of "making it" inscribed into its meritocratic ideal is limited by neoliberal notions of success: fulfilling career potentials, accumulating property, developing personal relationships and expressing identities through consumerist pursuits. It does not consider whether these aims are really universal, or whether some people may have valid alternate desires that would require extensive social change to realize. Nor does it question whether meritocracy is fair in the first place, or whether people who simply lack marketable personal attributes deserve a lesser standard of life.

Again, in outlining these positions, I do not claim that most people fit one or another of them exactly or that we can categorize the population according to these types. My aim is to get an idea of the various belief systems that support neoliberal ideals, and defining them in this way helps in getting to grips with their many facets. It is in fact likely that features of one may blend into features of another, and it is interesting to consider how the different contents of these positions coexist in society, as multiple responses to the background of neoliberalism that both complement and contrast one another. At a basic level, they are all intrinsically compatible because, ultimately, they support the existing social order by reproducing everyday routines of work and leisure, as opposed to acting against that demand to "enjoy responsibly." But at the level of specific beliefs too, they do not necessarily always clash, and it is worth considering how the different positions, and the games that represent them, both link together and work against each other.

As a beginning point, I have already mentioned that there is a kind of cynicism in the escapist defeatism of *NMH*, which shares traits with more obvious cynical self-interest in *GTAV*, while *SRIV*'s hedonism and *P5*'s reformism represent attempts to create an actual utopian ideal based on certain neoliberal parameters. Put differently, this can be seen as an opposition between "pessimistic" acceptance of the loss of clear meaning and the need to function within flawed circumstances, and an "optimistic" belief in making existing social relations work. But in other ways, *GTAV*'s cynical philosophy differs from that of *NMH*'s defeatism. First, *GTAV* validates a strong work ethic, according to which fulfilment and success are the result of effort, while *NMH* is an escape into entertainment that rejects work as anything but a necessary evil. In this respect, *GTAV* connects with *P5*'s acceptance of modern life demands, in which routine and responsibility are valued as the means to achieving satisfaction *alongside* moderate consumer pursuits, while *NMH* finds common ground with *SRIV*'s enjoyment focused rejection of laborious activity. Finally, in *GTAV* the existing social order is effectively accepted and celebrated as the best possible system, rather than resisted, or merely tolerated as in *NMH*. That is, in *NMH*, Travis still desires a way out that he cannot find, whereas the characters in *GTAV* embrace the demands of neoliberalism on their own terms despite their criticisms. Here, *SRIV* is similar to *GTAV*, as it also celebrates the modern conditions that enable consumerist freedoms of expression, and aims to erase the last vestiges of traditional authority. *P5*'s acceptance of the social order, conversely, is contingent on reform of current systems, and, like *NMH*, shows resentment for how things currently function through its stance on corruption and unjust distribution of opportunities. We can thus define the connections between the positions through three oppositions: Optimism-Pessimism; Responsibility-Enjoyment; Celebration-Resentment. *SRIV*'s hedonism is: Optimism, Enjoyment, Celebration; *GTAV*'s cynical self-interest is: Pessimism, Responsibility, Celebration; *NMH*'s escapist defeatism is: Pessimism, Enjoyment, Resentment; *P5*'s reformism is: Optimism, Responsibility, Resentment.

At the same time, these oppositions show how different psychological responses may relate to the neoliberal background ideology in a variety of ways that only partially internalize its ideals and demands. After all, a pure neoliberal position would be celebratory and optimistic and take the responsibility of tempering enjoyment, which none of these positions do. If these are only partial internalizations, then, they seem to accept neoliberal ideas *conditionally*, and even throw demands back at modern society. Indeed, each position contains an element that points beyond neoliberal capitalism even as it fails to really question the latter as a social system. *SRIV* rejects the notion of responsibility in the demand "enjoy responsibly" and, by taking very seriously the notion of self-actualization through enjoyment, effectively asks whether individual freedom must be tied to work. It does not consider how a society could function through hedonistic pleasure-seeking, but implies that the demand to work and pay for our pleasure is oppressive or surplus to requirements. *NMH* goes further here, as it rejects the whole work-leisure cycle and finds neoliberalized concepts of fulfilment and self-actualization to be meaningless. Although it fails to imagine an alternative mode of behaviour, because it is caught in isolated individualism, it suggests an undying desire to exist outside these dominant expectations and seek some meaningful goal. In *P5*, meanwhile, it is the notion of individual responsibility that is taken seriously, not only in terms of work but also in terms of a socially beneficial political participation. The result is a demand for a democracy in which people fully engage and their decisions actually matter. While it presents the issue largely as one of personal psychology and attitude, its motivating desire is for more social agency and widespread commitment to equal opportunities and justice. Finally, *GTAV* is the only one of these games to name capitalism as the root cause of social problems. It does so superficially, if not cynically, and only to submit that there is nothing to be done about it, but this naming and unsympathetic framing itself enables us to envisage the social formation as a particular, questionable system, rather than leaving it as that invisible background.

We can now imagine how a combination of the more critical or transcendent elements within the different ideological responses may create a more thoroughgoing social analysis. In effect, they present us with a perspective that can consider contradictions in the existing order, and resolutions that could engender potential alternative ways of organizing society. Such a perspective may, for example, contemplate whether the kinds of work we are generally obliged to do are socially necessary or personally fulfilling. It may ask whether the demand to "enjoy responsibly" by balancing ever growing work and consumer pressures actually constitutes a meaningful or coherent life goal, or whether alternative goals could be more satisfactory. It can also imagine the possibility of greater political engagement from the majority of people, and what it means to take collective responsibility for social conditions, rather than following individual desires. And if all these ideas are framed in relation to neoliberal capitalist systems of economics, politics and culture, they can even consider whether the systems as such produce demands that are inherently unrealistic, antagonistic and socially destructive.

The specific questions that then arise from such critical thinking are many and varied. For example, are there even enough jobs, especially satisfying, well-paid jobs, for everyone to do today? Is throwaway mass consumerism environmentally sustainable? Does an individualized focus on employment and consumerism detract from more meaningful social activity? Are the demands of globalized markets compatible with free and effective political decision-making? To what extent does corporate advertising, PR and lobbying help frame our political desires? And how might we need to change society to provide the kind of meaning, involvement and satisfaction we desire? If some of these questions seem overly radical even for progressives who perceive a need to address existing social problems, it should be clear by now that getting to the root of these problems may require re-evaluation of even the most deeply embedded assumptions about how societies work and how they could work. But it should also be clear that the fear of such self-critique and potential change is itself very much intertwined with the neoliberal ideology we are trying to interrogate, and the limitations it tries to place on collective agency.

Of course, none of these questions are explicitly articulated in the games I have explored, due to the ideological confines in which they operate. They merely come across in hints of contradiction or dissatisfaction, and often in fact in the games' failure to convincingly resolve the antagonisms they represent. It is their sense of incompleteness, rather than any political ideal, that functions as a demand for a deeper social critique and more convincing answers. In essence, the power of these cultural objects is in what they can't quite say, or what the representation of the city as a playground, battleground, wasteland or prison, and the conflict that creates, stand in for. Clearly these cities are not "realistic," but it is because of this we can ask why they are unrealistic in the particular way they are, and receive interesting and potentially significant answers.

Endnotes

1. Despite all the numbers in the titles which mark three of these games as parts of long-running series, only in one case (*Saints Row IV*) is there any significant narrative continuity from previous games. It is not uncommon for games to contain completely new characters and scenarios in each instalment of a series, with similar rules, structures and objectives creating the links between them.

2. Fredric Jameson, *The Geopolitical Aesthetic: Cinema and Space in the World System* (Bloomington, IN: Indiana University Press, 1992), p. 79.

3. Throughout this chapter I draw on ideas relating to neoliberalism developed by numerous social and cultural theorists, including: Zygmunt Bauman, Ulrich Beck, Wendy Brown, Jodi Dean, Mark Fisher, Fredric Jameson and Slavoj Žižek.

4. Ulrich Beck, *The Brave New World of Work* (Cambridge: Polity, 2000), p. 70.

5. Jodi Dean, *Democracy and Other Neoliberal Fantasies: Communicative Capitalism and Left Politics* (Durham, NC: Duke University Press, 2009), pp. 49-74.

6. Karl Marx, *The German Ideology* (New York: Prometheus, 1998), p. 67.

7. Jürgen Habermas, *Toward a Rational Society: Student Protest, Science, and Politics*, trans. by J. J. Shapiro (London: Heinemann Educational, 1971), p. 111.

8. Herbert Marcuse, *An Essay on Liberation* (Boston: Beacon, 1969), p. 11.

9. Jameson, 'The Antinomies of Postmodernity,' *The Cultural Turn: Selected Writings on the Postmodern, 1983-1998* (London: Verso, 1998), p. 50.

10. Marcuse, 'On Hedonism,' *Negations: Essays in Critical Theory*,

trans. by J. J. Shapiro (London: Allen Lane, 1968), p. 126.

11. This point is especially clear in *SRIII*, where the Saints have become a legitimate global brand with lucrative merchandizing deals, and sense that they have "sold out." But their response to corporate acceptance is merely to return to the pleasures of destructive, criminal acting out— precisely what was so marketable in the first place.

12. Some interesting perspectives on *Grand Theft Auto* in academic books and journals, many of which I draw on in this chapter, include: Paul Barrett, 'White Thumbs, Black Bodies: Race, Violence, and Neoliberal Fantasies in Grand Theft Auto: San Andreas,' *Review of Education, Pedagogy, and Cultural Studies*, 28:1, 2006, pp. 95-119; Ian Bogost, *Persuasive Games: The Expressive Power of Videogames* (Cambridge, MA: MIT, 2007); Nick Dyer-Witheford, and Greg de Peuter, *Games of Empire: Global Capitalism and Videogames* (Minneapolis, MN: University of Minnesota, 2009); Óliver Pérez Latorre, 'The Social Discourse of Video Games: Analysis Model and Case Study: GTA IV,' *Games and Culture*, 10.5, 2015, pp. 415-437; Miguel Sicart, *The Ethics of Computer Games* (Cambridge, MA: MIT, 2009).

13. Peter Sloterdijk, *Critique of Cynical Reason*, trans. by M. Eldred (Minneapolis, MN: University of Minnesota Press, 1987), p. 5.

14. Slavoj Žižek, *The Sublime Object of Ideology*, 2ⁿᵈ edn (London: Verso, 2008), p. 26.

15. Ibid., p, 30.

16. Jameson, *Postmodernism, or, The Cultural Logic of Late Capitalism* (London: Verso, 1991), p. 273.

17. Ibid., p. 6.

18. Ibid., p. 46.

19. Almost literally turning women into objects in some cases, such as in the private lap dance "game" in which the player can press buttons to "touch" the dancer, and get away with

it as long as the bouncer isn't looking. The woman herself has no voice or personality at all in this interaction.

20. *GTAV* is also one of an increasing number of modern games that introduces "micro transactions" into its in-game economy, which means allowing players in its online multiplayer mode to use real money to unlock items such as new cars or weapons instantly. The ethics of this practice is a subject in itself, but the interesting point here is that it seems to feed off the very ideology of competitive individualism and consumer desire the game fosters, and embodies not the detached counterculture vibe of its projected image, but that of the money-grabbing hipster corporations within its narrative.

21. Even less for the player, who can always switch to *GTAV*'s online mode, where all the main game's activities and more besides are open to competitive or co-operative play with other people.

22. Mark Fisher, *Capitalist Realism: Is There No Alternative?* (Winchester: O Books, 2009), pp. 22.

23. We learn that Travis's parents were murdered. At one point, Travis dismisses this as unimportant, but it is presumably a major factor contributing to his disconnection from society. He also holds onto a notion of vengeance for the murders, although it is hard to tell whether that is heartfelt or merely a concept he has absorbed from violent consumer entertainment.

24. Žižek, *The Ticklish Subject: The Absent Centre of Political Ontology*, 2nd edn (London: Verso, 2008), p. 481.

25. Dean, *Democracy and Other Neoliberal Fantasies*, p. 94.

26. The "shadows" in *P5* also refer to a Jungian term that denotes the hidden unconscious aspect of the personality, or the "dark side" which remains repressed and unrecognized by the conscious self.

27. The "trickster" is one of Jung's "archetypes," which are part

of the "collective unconscious," or potentials common to all human psyches that are given form in different cultures (in religion, myth, art and so on) or when assumed by an individual consciousness. The various shadows, Personas and arcana in *P5* also reference these archetypes.

28. Jameson, *The Geopolitical Aesthetic*, p. 31.
29. As with *GTAV*, the need to appeal to a certain audience is doubtless significant here. The main audience in this case being a Japanese youth strongly invested in consumer style and entertainment.
30. If we were to analyse this position in terms of another urban-set videogame, Sega's *Yakuza* series would be somewhat relevant, in the way it represents a traditional patriarchy in relation to the modern world. These Japanese gangster games split their play structures between the "masculinity" of the past and the "femininity" of mass consumer life. On one hand, there are the Yakuza themselves: a clearly defined hierarchy of men, bound by codes of conduct that must never be questioned no matter how arbitrary they seem, because they create a sense of order. On the other hand, there is the modern city, packed with bizarre (often sexualized) fads, fashions and technology, and oddball characters who seem almost childlike or lost. In this world, the Yakuza characters we play represent a grounded paternal force trying to reassert their ways among the chaos of maternal irrationality and decadence (which unconsciously, of course, they are completely obsessed with).

CULTURE, SOCIETY & POLITICS

Contemporary culture has eliminated the concept and public figure of the intellectual. A cretinous anti-intellectualism presides, cheerled by hacks in the pay of multinational corporations who reassure their bored readers that there is no need to rouse themselves from their stupor. Zer0 Books knows that another kind of discourse – intellectual without being academic, popular without being populist – is not only possible: it is already flourishing. Zer0 is convinced that in the unthinking, blandly consensual culture in which we live, critical and engaged theoretical reflection is more important than ever before.

If you have enjoyed this book, why not tell other readers by posting a review on your preferred book site.

Recent bestsellers from Zero Books are:

In the Dust of This Planet
Horror of Philosophy vol. 1
Eugene Thacker
In the first of a series of three books on the Horror of Philosophy,
In the Dust of This Planet offers the genre of horror as a way of
thinking about the unthinkable.
Paperback: 978-1-84694-676-9 ebook: 978-1-78099-010-1

Capitalist Realism
Is there no alternative?
Mark Fisher
An analysis of the ways in which capitalism has presented itself
as the only realistic political-economic system.
Paperback: 978-1-84694-317-1 ebook: 978-1-78099-734-6

Rebel Rebel
Chris O'Leary
David Bowie: every single song. Everything you want to know,
everything you didn't know.
Paperback: 978-1-78099-244-0 ebook: 978-1-78099-713-1

Cartographies of the Absolute
Alberto Toscano, Jeff Kinkle
An aesthetics of the economy for the twenty-first century.
Paperback: 978-1-78099-275-4 ebook: 978-1-78279-973-3

Malign Velocities
Accelerationism and Capitalism
Benjamin Noys
Long listed for the Bread and Roses Prize 2015, *Malign
Velocities* argues against the need for speed, tracking acceleration
as the symptom of the ongoing crises of capitalism.
Paperback: 978-1-78279-300-7 ebook: 978-1-78279-299-4

Meat Market
Female Flesh under Capitalism
Laurie Penny
A feminist dissection of women's bodies as the fleshy fulcrum of
capitalist cannibalism, whereby women are both consumers and
consumed.
Paperback: 978-1-84694-521-2 ebook: 978-1-84694-782-7

Poor but Sexy
Culture Clashes in Europe East and West
Agata Pyzik
How the East stayed East and the West stayed West.
Paperback: 978-1-78099-394-2 ebook: 978-1-78099-395-9

Romeo and Juliet in Palestine
Teaching Under Occupation
Tom Sperlinger
Life in the West Bank, the nature of pedagogy and the role of a
university under occupation.
Paperback: 978-1-78279-637-4 ebook: 978-1-78279-636-7

Sweetening the Pill
or How We Got Hooked on Hormonal Birth Control
Holly Grigg-Spall
Has contraception liberated or oppressed women? *Sweetening the Pill* breaks the silence on the dark side of hormonal contraception.
Paperback: 978-1-78099-607-3 ebook: 978-1-78099-608-0

Why Are We The Good Guys?
Reclaiming your Mind from the Delusions of Propaganda
David Cromwell
A provocative challenge to the standard ideology that Western power is a benevolent force in the world.
Paperback: 978-1-78099-365-2 ebook: 978-1-78099-366-9

Readers of ebooks can buy or view any of these bestsellers by clicking on the live link in the title. Most titles are published in paperback and as an ebook. Paperbacks are available in traditional bookshops. Both print and ebook formats are available online.
Find more titles and sign up to our readers' newsletter
at http://www.johnhuntpublishing.com/culture-and-politics
Follow us on Facebook
at https://www.facebook.com/ZeroBooks
and Twitter at https://twitter.com/Zer0Books